T0273531

"The Practicing Change Series is compelling and immediately applicable. Each book weaves us through story, illustration, and discussion to contextualize paradigm-shifting frameworks for thinking. Your leadership, but more importantly the impact through your leadership, will experience a trajectory change through the words penned. Tod is a master storyteller, carefully threading points, principles, and processes with ease and nuance. Today's era of leadership calls for continual, on-the-go growth, and this series offers solutions to today's demands. For the leader whose time is limited and responsibilities toward self and service are complex, these books are for you."

Wendy Nolasco, general supervisor and vice president of US Mission for the Foursquare Church

"If only trust were enough. But as Tod Bolsinger points out in *Invest in Transformation*, while trust is an important resource, it is most valuable not when it is stockpiled for personal security but when it is invested in transformation. For leaders who are willing to step courageously into adaptive challenges, Bolsinger provides a clear and concise (although certainly not easy) guide for developing the perspective and skill sets needed to effectively lead organizational change. This is a book I will return to again and again."

Angie Ward, director of the Doctor of Ministry Program and associate professor of leadership and ministry at Denver Seminary

"It has been said that 'Trust is built in drops and lost in buckets.' In his slender-yet-substantive book *Invest in Transformation*, Tod Bolsinger helpfully weds transformation and trust. Furthermore, he offers valuable counsel on how the two might be synced and mutually reinforcing. In an effort to be and to do better as a leader, I have found the work of Bolsinger to be invaluable. Along with many others, I am grateful for his practical, actionable insights on leadership and for his graceful, enjoyable prose."

Todd Still, DeLancey Dean and Hinson Professor of Christian Scriptures at George W. Truett Theological Seminary, Baylor University

"Leaders who know organizational change is needed but don't know how to go about it will find accessible, practical, and wise guidance in Tod Bolsinger's Practicing Change Series. I've found the concepts of adaptive leadership incredibly helpful in thinking through organizational challenges. Bolsinger helps us apply and practice these concepts in a way that will transform our organizations and ourselves as leaders."

Teri McDowell Ott, editor and publisher of the *Presbyterian Outlook* and author of *Necessary Risks: Challenges Privileged People Need to Face*

"The Practicing Change Series provides exactly the kind of help that busy leaders need in seeking to bring meaningful change to their organizations in the midst of the ongoing demands of day-to-day leadership. Concisely accessible. Imminently practical. Immediately actionable. And built on solid theory tested in the real world. My own life and leadership have been profoundly impacted by having Tod Bolsinger as a trusted guide in navigating the complexity of leading adaptive change."

Barry D. Jones, senior pastor of Irving Bible Church and author of *Dwell: Life with God for the World*

"Every maturing leader fears irrelevance. In response, most work harder at the practices that made them successful in the first place. Tod Bolsinger thinks that's a bad idea, and he's right. Through four small books, Bolsinger offers us pure gold: practical ways for leaders to keep their skills on pace with inevitable and rapid change. *Invest in Transformation*, one of the four books, is a worthy read. It encourages leaders to embrace adaptive leadership practices, offers insights on navigating the challenges of organizational change, and recommends investing trust to drive successful transformation."

Randy Remington, president of The Foursquare Church

"Tod Bolsinger understands and loves leaders, and he understands and loves churches, and he knows change is hard. In this book, he sits down next to us as a wise friend and talks us through the mental models and practical skills we need to adapt to the world as it is and as it will be, giving us a map for investing in deep change just in time."

Trisha Taylor, author of *The Leader's Journey: Answering the Call to Personal and Congregational Transformation*

Invest in Transformation

Quit Relying on Trust

TOD BOLSINGER

Foreword by Marty Linsky
Illustrated by Mark Demel

An imprint of InterVarsity Press
Downers Grove, Illinois

To Jim Osterhaus, Steve Yamaguchi, and Terry Looper—

with gratitude for your coaching and

mentoring in my own life.

InterVarsity Press
P.O. Box 1400 | Downers Grove, IL 60515-1426
ivpress.com | email@ivpress.com

©2024 by Tod E. Bolsinger

All rights reserved. No part of this book may be reproduced in any form without written permission from InterVarsity Press.

InterVarsity Press® is the publishing division of InterVarsity Christian Fellowship/USA®. For more information, visit intervarsity.org.

All Scripture quotations, unless otherwise indicated, are taken from The Holy Bible, New International Version®, NIV®. Copyright © 1973, 1978, 1984, 2011 by Biblica, Inc.™ Used by permission of Zondervan. All rights reserved worldwide. www.zondervan.com. The "NIV" and "New International Version" are trademarks registered in the United States Patent and Trademark Office by Biblica, Inc.™

While any stories in this book are true, some names and identifying information may have been changed to protect the privacy of individuals.

Illustrations by Mark Demel.

Published in association with Helmers Literary Services.

The publisher cannot verify the accuracy or functionality of website URLs used in this book beyond the date of publication.

Cover design: David Fassett
Interior design: Jeanna Wiggins

ISBN 978-1-5140-0872-0 (print) | ISBN 978-1-5140-0873-7 (digital)

Printed in the United States of America ∞

Library of Congress Cataloging-in-Publication Data
A catalog record for this book is available from the Library of Congress.

30   29   28   27   26   25   24 | 8   7   6   5   4   3   2   1

CONTENTS

FOREWORD BY MARTY LINSKY

I am writing this flying home to New York after four days in Los Angeles with my fifty-two-year-old son, Sam, and his wife, son, and mother-in-law.

The weekend ended with a long unplanned, intimate conversation between Sam and me in front of a fireplace in the lobby of my hotel. Without naming it, we talked about what we both needed to do in this last chapter of my life to enrich our already deep relationship and make the best use of whatever time we have left together.

I experienced it as a hard, complicated, important, and generative conversation, requiring us each to voice and then try to let go of perspectives and assumptions—"truths" that we were inured to and had worked for us. We agreed to individually abandon some habituated ways of thinking and being, and to experiment with some new behaviors.

Then I read Tod Bolsinger's *How Not to Waste a Crisis*.

Sam and I were modeling the very process Tod describes.

Tod brings a spiritual anchor and a lifetime of addressing concrete problems to the connective work of applying the tools and frameworks of adaptive leadership to the vagaries of everyday personal and professional life, especially relevant in times characterized by constant, rapid change.

No matter who you are, where you are, how you spend your days, or how old you are, Tod Bolsinger's practical guidance and probing reflective questions are a vehicle for you and your organization, family, or community to get off the dance floor, get on the balcony, bring a new perspective to the challenges and opportunities in front of you, and begin to make more progress than you have in the past in closing the gap between your most noble aspirations and your current reality.

He has given us a gift. I am already a beneficiary.

ABOUT THE PRACTICING CHANGE SERIES

The Practicing Change books are about learning skills for leading in a time of deep disruption and change. Together, through them all, we will learn to recognize and then reset our leadership skills for a world that is constantly being upset and reset.

First, we will learn to see the out-of-date habits that have been cultivated through our successes. Then, we will work on new skills necessary for leading in times of change. Those new skills will enable us to embody a different form of leadership—what is called "adaptive leadership."

Adaptive leadership, as developed by Ronald Heifetz and Marty Linsky, is an approach to organizational problems that is needed when your old best practices no longer work. Adaptive leadership starts with diagnosis: Is this problem something that our expertise can solve or not? Is this something that requires us to apply a solution that already exists, or does it fall outside of our current knowledge and ability? Will it require learning and making really hard no-win choices?[1] As we shall repeatedly see, developing adaptive capacity—

that is, the capacity to apply and adapt an organization's most sacred core values so that its mission will thrive in this new environment—is the greatest challenge of leadership.[2]

Most communities are hardwired to resist this kind of adaptation. They believe that survival means reinforcing the way we have always done things in the past. The result is that instead of undergoing transformation in order to be more effective in their mission to serve the world, organizations unconsciously reinforce the very status quo that is not working.

> **Instead of undergoing transformation in order to be more effective in their mission to serve the world, organizations unconsciously reinforce the very status quo that is not working.**

Schools want to attract students to maintain the faculty who have come to do research within the safety of tenure and the resources of an academic community. A nonprofit's work that was once an innovative solution to a real problem becomes, after a time, an institution whose own survival is now the core purpose for being. In order to restore their flagging attendance or lagging donations, churches double down on the programs that people have historically loved most and will fill the facilities that they invested in building. And established businesses get disrupted by upstart startups while they are busy picking out new furniture for a bigger corporate office.

When a changing world or changing needs require an organization, institution, or company to itself change in order to keep being relevant to the challenges that are arising around them, it becomes clear that the internal organizational transformation needed—and the losses that must be faced—is an even more difficult leadership challenge than the external reason for changing.

This requires learning a new set of leadership practices.

In these four books *(How Not to Waste a Crisis, The Mission Always Wins, Leading Through Resistance,* and *Invest in Transformation)* we are going to reexamine four "mindsets" that have resulted in bad habits for most leaders. We'll take on one of them through each book:

1. Trying harder at what has been successful in the past

2. Focusing on pleasing our historical stakeholders

3. Doing whatever we can to eliminate resistance

4. Confusing trust with transformation

These mindsets are so ingrained within most leaders that they are usually never questioned. Shouldn't we work hard, take care of our most loyal members, manage resistance to change, and be trustworthy?

Yes. But also no. Not primarily.

Your primary work as a leader is to develop your own capacity to lead your people through the transformation necessary to face the challenges of a changing world.

And that takes practice. Lots of practice. Hours of deliberate practice.

Feel free to read these books in any order, starting with the "old mindset" that is most familiar or potentially most challenging for you. In each book, we will start with a problem area, and then instead of trying to learn a new intellectual concept, we'll focus instead on a new *skill*—trusting that that new skill will help us both see and think differently.[3] If we can keep practicing the new skill (and reinforcing the new insight), eventually we'll develop new habits that will become second nature.

> Your primary work as a leader is to develop your own capacity to lead your people through the transformation necessary to face the challenges of a changing world.

The pattern that we will use in these books will be the same. We will start with a case study adapted from real-life leadership challenges.[4] After the case study (and throughout the book) we will pause and engage in some reflective exercises that are very similar to the kinds of coaching conversations that my team and I have with leaders all over the world.

These are called "balcony sessions."[5]

While the "dance floor" is where the action is, the "balcony" is where leaders try to get some larger perspective amid the swirl of the challenges in front of them, decisions foisted on them, opinions and desires of everyone around them, and even their own conflicting internal feelings.[6] Good leaders learn how to toggle back and forth between "listening on the

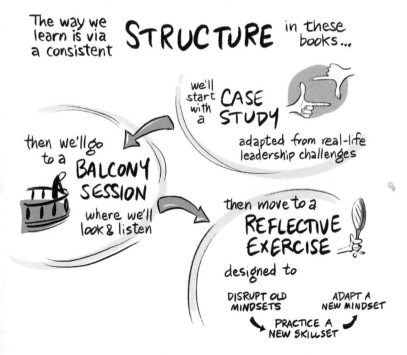

The way we learn is via a consistent **STRUCTURE** in these books...

we'll start with a **CASE STUDY**
adapted from real-life leadership challenges

then we'll go to a **BALCONY SESSION** where we'll look & listen

then move to a **REFLECTIVE EXERCISE** designed to

DISRUPT OLD MINDSETS

ADAPT A NEW MINDSET

PRACTICE A NEW SKILLSET

dance floor" and "looking from the balcony" and begin to see a different way of approaching a new challenge.

After the first balcony session, we will proceed through a reflective-practice learning process:

1. Disrupting an old mindset (which leads to)

2. Practicing a new skillset (which leads to)

3. Embodying an adaptive reset (a new habit for adaptive leadership)

The Practicing Change books—and the process that they teach us—are the ultimate survival guide for leaders in chaos. Together we unlearn bad habits, master adaptive skills, and embrace a leadership style that offers genuine change and transformation—to our people and ourselves.

INTRODUCTION
TRUST & TRANSFORMATION

There is no transformation without trust. Period. End of sentence.

That axiom is as bedrock and foundational to leading as it can be.

If you are a leader reading this book, I encourage you to pause here and internalize this truth before you read anything else. If nothing else, taking this truth seriously is critical because of the number of scandals of untrustworthy leaders and what it has done in our culture—even in the church.

If you are reading this book because you have been entrusted with the calling to bring about good, healthy, missional change, you should pause even a bit longer and be as honest as possible with yourself about what kind of trust it is going to take to accomplish your leadership vision:

→ The need for you to be diligent about your character

→ The obligation for you to be consistent in your integrity

→ The candor, courage, and empathy to walk with a group through the disruption of change

→ The absolute necessity for you to be honest about your shortcomings (because they will be exposed!)

Leaders don't have to be perfect, but they do have to be trustworthy. When trust ebbs, leading people to accomplish any mission is almost impossible. If leaders are not trusted, no one will follow them anywhere.

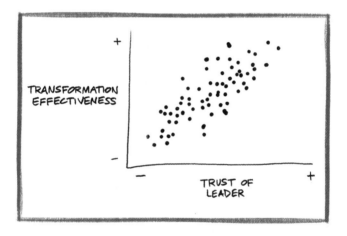

Even more, if a leadership challenge was thrust on you because of an external disruption—a rapidly changing world, a crisis, or a radical change in the environment or context of your mission—then the anxiety caused by the unknown requires that trust to be even greater, because the unknown and unfamiliar requires deep personal *transformation*. Transformation is the crux of all leadership challenges.

> When trust is gone,
> the transformational journey is over.

LEADERSHIP AND TRANSFORMATION

Leadership, as I define it, is *energizing a community of people toward their own transformation so that they can accomplish a shared mission*.[1] And that transformation cannot begin until the level of trust is high enough for the group to even consider what it will cost to be transformed.

Adaptive change requires leaders to face the challenges of a changing world or disrupted environment with hard decisions around core values, with hard questions about what we need to learn (and unlearn!), and with hard truths about the necessity of our own transformation. Adaptive change requires leaders to become what they are not yet already.

Transformation is what makes adaptive leadership *adaptive*.

> Transformation is the crux of
> all leadership challenges.

Adaptive leadership inspires and equips people to see beyond their own personal goals, security, and visions of success to collaborate to bring about the change necessary for the organization to thrive in a different (and often disruptive) environment.

Since this is not at all natural, the transformation process requires leaders to "keep the work at the center of people's attention," and to pace and structure the change process so there is time for the members of the organization to absorb the changes, the losses they must face, and the transformation needed.[2]

Like a chef trying to slowly sauté onions so that they will become softened, browned, and flavorful without sticking or burning, the leader must continually pay attention, adjust the heat, and every now and then stir the pot to keep the process going.

A group facing challenges requires deep transformation into the very best version of who they can possibly be.

"Leadership is disappointing your own people at a rate they can absorb," Marty Linsky told an interviewer when describing the challenges of adaptive leadership.[3] And whenever I quote the line in a seminar or speaking engagement, it always gets a laugh and a lot of nodding heads.

Leaders recognize themselves—and the challenges confronting them—in this statement. They understand now, if they didn't when they took the job, that unlike being a manager who fixes problems, sorts out solutions, makes plans that align, and allocates resources (and thus make people happy!), leaders often are faced with taking people through a process of personal and organizational transformation in order to face these disruptive challenges in front of them.

ADAPTIVE CHALLENGES...

1. REQUIRE LEARNING

2. RESULT IN FACING LOSS

3. REVEAL COMPETING VALUES THAT MUST BE NAMED & NAVIGATED

4. REQUIRE EXPERIMENTATION & FAILURE

5. RESULT IN RESISTANCE THAT MUST BE FACED WITH RESILIENCE

It is a process that they often resist and a reality that makes leading any group of people really hard. To be sure, when we took on a leadership challenge, we naturally assumed that there would be challenges and that some days would be hard. ("It's the hard that makes it great!" as Tom Hanks's gruff baseball manager character in *A League of Their Own* said.) But what most of us didn't expect is how hard it would become *to lead the very people who asked you to step into the leadership role.* We didn't really expect to have to face resistance and even opposition from the staff, partners, and board members who asked us to take on the challenge. We figured they would have our backs and that they were ready for the rough road ahead.

Until we realized that they weren't.

The often subconscious expectation of our people was that we would make things better *for them*. We would "right the ship" or "trim the sails" or get us going "full steam ahead." They may have expected that there would be some rough seas, but mostly they assumed that our leadership would make an organization (one they belong to and have invested in) a more efficient and effective version of what it already is. The hard news to deliver is that a group facing challenges requires deep transformation into the very best version of who they can possibly be—transformation that requires people to endure *loss*.

Those losses are not just cosmetic but go to the level of personal and organizational identity:

→ Reevaluating legacy commitments

→ Reconsidering unspoken loyalties

→ Shifting unquestioned behaviors and attitudes

→ Especially: naming and navigating competing values

Adaptive leadership confronts the gaps in what we *say* we believe and what we actually *do* each day. It queries people on where they need to grow and what they need to learn.

And most painfully, adaptive leadership asks people to face what they must leave behind in order to move the organization forward into uncharted territory.

CHANGE AND LOSS

"People don't resist change, they resist loss," Heifetz and Linsky have taught us.[4]

And this reality helps us better understand the most delicate skill required of change leaders: to utilize both empathy and courage to shape the "disappointment" of your own people . . . *at a rate they can absorb*, as Linsky so memorably put it. To bring about transformation without losing all trust from your people, to pace the transformation in a way that will enable you to invest the trust you have in the process, ultimately leads to your organization becoming people who can face the necessary losses and take on the challenges in front of them.

> Adaptive leadership asks people
> to face what they must leave behind
> in order to move the organization
> forward into uncharted territory.

That's what this book is about. It is about learning the skill set and developing the *adaptive* mindset that moves from trust to transformation. Together we will learn how . . .

→ to build a high-trust account that you can invest in transformation;

→ to work collaboratively to restore trust when your change processes have (understandably!) depleted it . . . so you can then invest again in transformation;

→ to then restore it again and invest again; and

→ to repeat.

These steps require us to understand even more deeply the dance between trust and transformation—and how desiring to be considered a trustworthy leader can keep us from being a transformational one.

CHAPTER 1
A LEADERSHIP STORY:
AFTER THE GALA

That's nice, **she thought** as she sipped her coffee at the corner table of her favorite café and skimmed again through the texts and emails that had come in during the night.

Alison Grant told herself that it was pretty vain to be re-reading the accolades that had filled her inbox, but that didn't stop her from doing so.

No one! No one, Alison, but YOU could have pulled this off. What an amazing turnaround! ☺ ☺ ☺

You are a gift to us, Dr. Grant! You rock! Thank you for everything.

That was an amazing celebration, Ali. You deserved all the accolades and more!

She broke off a small bite of the muffin on the plate in front of her. Since she had spent a lot more hours taking to heart all of the negative comments of the past few years, basking in some affirmation didn't seem too far out of balance.

"So, how does it feel to be the most celebrated leader in the history of our organization?" said the gruff but warm voice behind her.

She shoved her phone aside and turned to greet him, hoping that her board chair and mentor hadn't seen the screen as he walked up to the table. "Thanks, Bob. Last night was . . . really something. It's almost embarrassing. You and the board really didn't need to make such a big deal out of it. 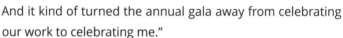 And it kind of turned the annual gala away from celebrating our work to celebrating me."

"You deserve it, Alison. Without you, there would be no work to celebrate. With so many people of faith so caught up in the political conflict about climate change, we were desperate. Without you, Environmental Advocates would have closed our doors months ago. The donations would have completely dried up, the staff would have given up, and the earth—well—the earth would burn up!"

He smiled a bit sheepishly as he sat down across from her. "Last night was simply the board's way of telling you that we appreciate all that you have done. You changed the narrative, brought back the donors, and restored trust. We're absolutely confident that with you at the helm, our work will make a difference for years to come."

His eyes darted to catch the attention of the waiter for some coffee. "Next month, I think the board might be ready to hear your ideas about the strategic planning process you've wanted us to take on. I think we'll have a nice discussion."

Alison glanced down at the menu, feeling her stomach turn just a bit. If they knew what she was really thinking, they might take back that award.

When she arrived at the small Environmental Advocates office an hour later, she was surprised to see that her executive assistant, Yuri Bae, was there. The small team had all been given a long weekend after the multiple late nights prepping for the gala, and she had been looking forward to having some time to reflect in an empty office.

"Hey, Yuri! What are you doing here this morning?"

Yuri looked up from her desk. "Oh, somebody needs to make the bank deposit for the donations from last night," she said with less enthusiasm than Alison would have expected after the success of the gala.

Alison poured herself a cup of coffee and walked over to Yuri's desk. "You know that could wait until Monday, right? You deserve to take an extra day for yourself. That celebration and all of those embarrassingly nice things people said about me were as much for you." She paused until Yuri looked up from her work, making eye contact. "You do know that I couldn't do any of this without you."

Yuri returned her attention to her computer screen. "Yes. Well, I was going to wait until Monday to tell you this, but now that the gala is over and with things going so well . . . it seems like a good time for me to move on. You can get someone else to do this role easily, I'd think, after last night."

Alison was too shocked to reply.

"I'm sorry to tell you this today, Ali, and I don't want to take away from all the well-earned praise for you, but Earth First has been after me about their open associate director role. I've been putting them off, but after the event last night it just felt like I've done all I can do here, and I'm ready for the next step. I have an interview with them on Monday. I just wanted to make sure you heard that from me."

Alison dropped into a chair. "I'm stunned, Yuri. Is it more money? More responsibility? You're already so much more than an executive assistant; you know that. You practically *are* my associate director. Do you want the title? I can talk to the board about that. I mean, you're going to be at the center of the new strategic plan—"

"Plan? What plan?" Yuri's voice ticked up a notch. "Wasn't that what we were supposed to launch last night? I didn't hear any-thing about a new plan. The whole team was waiting for your speech. The whole evening had been choreographed for you to lay out for the donors the urgency of the need and for the next chapter of our work. But nothing. Not a word. The plan vanished in the cascade of balloons and tributes. Set aside when the praise for your trusted leadership was piling on."

Alison's gut wrenched again. "C'mon, Yuri. You knew about that surprise, but I didn't. I was thrown off. It felt weird making a big announcement about charting a new course when everyone was celebrating that we had survived the storm."

Yuri shook her head. "The storm was over a year ago. This was the moment when we were going to look to the future and use the annual fundraising gala to lay the groundwork for Environmental Advocates to become more than an educational organization."

Yeah. She knew that. But . . .

"We worked on your speech for weeks. Remember? 'If we are going to truly make an impact as an environmental organization, we can't just support people of faith who are scientists and science teachers, we have to get everyone involved. The environment needs advocates in the lab and the classroom, but also the courtroom and the board room. The environment needs advocates who are artists and poets, pastors and theologians, business leaders and civil servants, soccer moms and Supreme Court justices. We need people of genuine faith who have studied the science and believe that it is an act of Christian witness to care for creation. We need true environmental advocates in every sector of society.' Remember?"

Alison clasped her hands together to keep them from trembling. "Yes, of course, I remember, but—"

"We all worked on it for months, Ali. We had everything ready to go and then it turned into a 'Celebration of Ali's Steady Hand at the Wheel.'"

"But that wasn't my idea—it was the board's, right? What was I supposed to do? Everyone was talking about how much they trusted me and how grateful they were that we were back on course. The balloons, the flowers, the slide show. It was a lot."

"It was ten minutes of a two-hour event." Yuri was now looking right at Ali, unblinking. "The surprise was just supposed to be one part of the evening. The board insisted we do it. It was even Bob's idea! He thought that before we talk about any new direction, we should celebrate how far we have come. But all we did was look back. You were supposed to share the vision of the future . . . and you didn't."

Alison sighed. "It just seemed out of place. And yes, I have to admit that it really felt good at that moment to hear all of the praise. Do you remember how bad those first two years were? I could barely sleep most nights as we tried to turn this ship around. So, yeah. I probably basked in the affection last night. It's nice to be affirmed and trusted."

"Of course, you did! You deserve every bit of it. You are the most trusted leader I know right now. But that is exactly why we needed you to shape the narrative of our next initiative. You said it yourself: 'We have to become an organization that puts faith and science to work actually changing hearts and minds.' This was going to be your big moment and your 'I Have a Dream Speech' and instead it became your 'Sally Fields at the Oscars Moment'—'You like me, you really like me.'"

Alison stared at her, feeling her face flush. "That's not fair! I didn't ask for the award. And you and I both know that the donors are going to struggle with the direction. They want an environmental organization that is purely educational, and this plan is going to seem too . . . political. It's touchy. It will take time and pacing, it will take—"

"Courage! Courage, Ali. It will take courage to put your trust on the line for the change that we need to make. We had everything ready to go, but you didn't tee up the change."

Ali tried to lower the heat in the room. "I didn't do it *yet*. I just saw Bob this morning. He wants me to share my ideas with the board next month. I was just trying to navigate the evening."

Yuri shook her head again. "You pulled your punch. You knew that it was going to be controversial with the donors, and you didn't want to put a damper on the big celebration of your trusted leadership. Bob knew what he was doing, Ali. You know he doesn't believe the donors will back the new plan, and he sabotaged the announcement by making the evening about you. Once they gave you that award, they had you."

"Do you really think that's all it was?" Ali asked, unable to keep the hurt out of her voice. "Was it really all just Bob manipulating me so that I wouldn't make the announcement?"

Yuri softened. "No, no. All of us, including Bob, really do celebrate all that you have done. You really did bring us back from the brink, and we're here today because of your leadership. You deserve everything you got last night. And you know that I was cheering the loudest. You are a trusted leader who has done an amazing job."

"But . . ." Alison drew out the word, waiting for the shoe to drop.

"But you've said it yourself, Ali. What got us here won't take us where we need to go. And the fact that we have been successful

so far means that we'll have harder decisions to make and will face resistance—especially from the old-guard board and our more traditional donors. I don't think there are going to be as many bouquets of flowers and balloon sprays."

Ali tried to hold back a small grin. "We? I thought you were leaving."

Yuri picked at her fingernails while a sheepish smile flickered across her face. "Well, I might be. I'm not sure, actually. I do love it here and I really believe in where we are trying to go."

Yuri's smile evaporated as she held Alison's gaze. "But do you have the stomach to take on Bob and bring the board along?"

BALCONY SESSION

1 PUT YOURSELF IN ALISON GRANT'S EMOTIONAL FRAME of MIND FROM the NARRATIVE. BASED on WHAT SHE had BEEN THROUGH to TURN the ORGANIZATION AROUND, HOW MIGHT SHE have BEEN FEELING ABOUT the ACCOLADES & ATTENTION SHE RECEIVED?

2 WHAT do YOU IMAGINE SHE was FEELING DURING the DIFFICULT CONVERSATION WITH YURI?

3 HOW WOULD YOU DESCRIBE the INNER CONFLICT WITHIN ALISON ABOUT WHAT WILL be REQUIRED of HER to BOTH WORK WITH the BOARD & KEEP GOOD TEAMMATES LIKE YURI?

BOARD

MATES

CHAPTER 2
OLD MINDSET:
SECURE LEADERS MAINTAIN A BIG TRUST ACCOUNT

Writing in the wake of the 9/11 bombings, leadership expert and author Margaret Wheatley responded to the question of how leaders and teams could learn to plan ahead when the world was so volatile. How might leaders get better at predicting what the future will bring?

She waved the question aside.

You can't predict the future, Wheatley wrote, but "it is possible to prepare for the future without knowing what it will be. The primary way to prepare for the unknown is to attend to the quality of our relationships, to how well we know and trust one another."[1]

If that answer leaves you with a heaviness in your heart, you are not alone. Trust in organizations, institutions—even trust in neighbors—has been declining at a rate that many previously thought unthinkable.[2] Even more, the lack of trust in leaders—either political, institutional, corporate, even religious—led one author to write about "the scandal of leadership."[3]

When the books don't balance, the public and private messages don't align, the decisions made seem more for personal gain than for the organizational good, trust evaporates quickly. Psychologist and executive coach Jim Osterhaus explains that while trust increases from the congruence of leaders repeatedly doing what they say, the trust level goes down when the words and actions don't match. According to Osterhaus, "Trust is gained like a thermostat and lost like a light switch." A leader builds trust slowly over time by constantly monitoring the conditions and actions that create the "climate" of trust in the room. But even one action, if perceived as incongruent, can make the levels of trust plummet into darkness.[4]

When trust has fallen to the place where leading anywhere is impossible, there is nothing else to do except restore it. For

example, when an institution wants to embark on a building renovation project, if there is no money in the bank, then the renovation work must stop. The bank account of trust needs to be replenished.

To restore the trust account, a leader needs both

technical competence and relational congruence.[5] Technical competence is the sense that leaders are doing everything within their power and their job description to be as effective as possible. Before they can call a group to change and grow, leaders must demonstrate that they have the ability to serve the needs of their charges right where they are. Before they call people to take on the challenges of the uncharted territory in front of them, they must demonstrate that they can ably navigate the most basic expectations they have been authorized to accomplish. Before an organization will even *consider* undergoing costly change, there must be a sense that the leadership is doing its job. Because change is so potentially painful, therefore, transformational leadership then does not *begin* with transformation.

It begins in *competence*.

Now, certainly, if technical competence is the *only* criteria for leadership, it can lead to significant problems (numerous scandals led by "the smartest people in the room" immediately come to mind), so genuine trust in leadership is more than just credibility that comes from *technical competence*; it also requires *relational congruence*.

Relational congruence is the way that leaders show up for the people "entrusted to their care."[6] Relational congruence is the personal capacity—the emotional intelligence, the moral character, the ability to listen and communicate—to uphold values and protect the relationships, the integrity, and the culture of the organization. When leaders function with relational congruence, they strengthen the bonds, deepen the affection, and create the wellspring of trust needed to face the unknown challenges of a changing and disrupted world.[7]

When leaders have high credibility and high trust, they

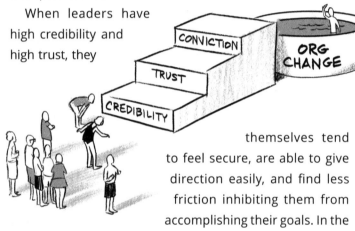

themselves tend to feel secure, are able to give direction easily, and find less friction inhibiting them from accomplishing their goals. In the words of Stephen M. R. Covey, "Nothing is as fast as the speed of trust," and "once you create trust—genuine character-based and competence-based trust—almost everything else falls into place."[8]

WHEN TRUST IS NOT ENOUGH

It is completely understandable, then, for leaders to assume that their main responsibility is to build a big trust

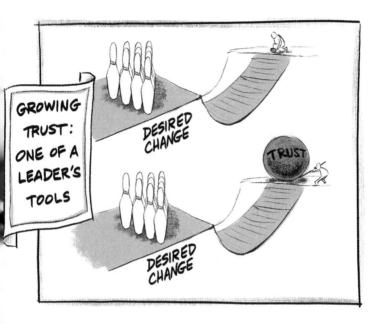

account—that building and maintaining trust is the most important part of their leadership responsibilities. It also makes sense for leaders to believe that the most important metric of their success is the degree to which they are trusted by the key people in the organization. Like a bank account, when the "trust fund" is high, the leader is succeeding; when trust declines, the leader's own performance is declining. Right?

Or . . . have we misunderstood what leadership is really all about?

Leadership is not managing the current resources and culture of the organization to keep the business going. That is management. Management is a critical and important task. (And good management is critical to high trust!) It is not beneath leadership in the hierarchy of importance, it is just a different task than leadership, with a different objective.

Management is taking care of the people, priorities, and resources "entrusted to your care" and executing on the plan and goals that you have been authorized to take on. Management maintains high trust because management has a big agenda, a long to-do list, a set of critical objectives and key results that have to be executed on and accomplished.[9] Management, according to John Kotter, is "about coping with complexity."[10] It is about getting the various goals and groups, factions and facts, commitments and conditions, products and processes aligned and functioning well together.

Management is about *coping with complexity. Leadership* is about *navigating change.*

> ## Have we misunderstood what leadership is really all about?

Leadership is measured by the transformation of a people who are facing challenges that require change. Leaders for a time of change and disruption, then, should not be measured just by high trust, but instead by organizational missional transformation. It is a process that is often marked by the need to address challenges for which there are no easy answers nor best practices.

This kind of leadership—adaptive leadership—requires the group to let go of historic biases, legacy commitments, and the trusted strategies of the past; to navigate competing values, experiment, and face failures; and to demonstrate resilience in the face of resistance.

In other words, if taking the Israelites to the Promised Land had just been a management problem, then they would have been able to navigate the wilderness in about six weeks, but as an adaptive leadership challenge, it took forty years. For the once-enslaved people of God to become a new nation that could live freely and offer an example of hope and witness to the world would require the kind of deep spiritual makeover that would disrupt most of their expectations when they were freed on that night of Passover.

> **Leaders for a time of change and disruption should not be measured just by high trust, but instead by organizational missional transformation.**

Truly transformational leadership, then,

→ *begins* in technical competence: the skills and abilities that serve, manage, and preserve the organization and its current work;

→ is *validated* in relational congruence, that is, the character, care, and constancy that creates the organizational health and personal trust that enables people to stay together even when things go awry; and

→ *becomes transformational* through adaptive capacity, that is, the ability to wisely shift (and sometimes leave behind!) values, attitudes, and behaviors in order to grow and discover solutions to the greatest challenges brought on by a changing world.[11]

So, let's be doubly clear-headed about what can be a daunting reality.

There is no transformation without trust.

But trust is not transformation.

Deep transformation requires a high degree of trust. But that trust alone doesn't bring transformation. Leading change requires trust to be *invested* in transformation. Trust cannot be stockpiled for a leader's own personal security, and it certainly cannot be squandered for a leader's own personal comfort and status. Trust is a valuable commodity that must be utilized wisely and well in a deep process of personal and organizational transformation.

So, then, how do we go about investing trust for transformation? *Through taking on actual adaptive challenges together.*

IDENTITY, CALLING, AND TRANSFORMATION

When we describe this adaptive process with faith leaders, we use a diagram that is focused around two big questions.

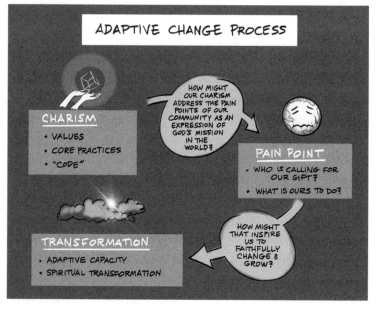

ADAPTIVE CHANGE PROCESS

CHARISM
• VALUES
• CORE PRACTICES
• "CODE"

HOW MIGHT OUR CHARISM ADDRESS THE PAIN POINTS OF OUR COMMUNITY AS AN EXPRESSION OF GOD'S MISSION IN THE WORLD?

PAIN POINT
• WHO IS CALLING FOR OUR GIFT?
• WHAT IS OURS TO DO?

HOW MIGHT THAT INSPIRE US TO FAITHFULLY CHANGE & GROW?

TRANSFORMATION
• ADAPTIVE CAPACITY
• SPIRITUAL TRANSFORMATION

These questions are demanding. They require us to reflect on our organizational identity, our sense of missional calling, and the necessity of transformation that is at the heart of adaptive work.

We'll take the time to unpack them in detail, but for now, notice how these questions are not the kinds that can be solved easily or even individually by one gifted authority figure. Notice how they require discernment, collaboration, and tough decisions.

The two questions are these:

→ How might our charism address the pain points of our community as an expression of God's mission in the world?

→ How might that inspire us to faithfully change and grow?

These questions focus attention on what is most important about our organization (the gift of our values and identity, which come from the history and identity that make each organization unique, or what we call an organizational *charism*), what point of pain in our community or world is calling for our charism, and the deep change needed for our organization to live out that calling in the world.

As a team works together on the kinds of problems and tasks inspired by questions like these, they are stretched beyond their best practices, they are required to acknowledge a lack of expertise, and they must face the reality that they will likely have to let go of a lot of what they have historically depended on. In confronting these questions and the trans-formation needed, they slowly develop *adaptive capacity*— the capacity to apply and adapt their most sacred core values so that their mission will thrive in this new environment.[12]

When a team works together on these questions with *enough* trust in the leadership and in the group as a whole to begin to identify and confront these larger, underlying, adaptive challenges, then the team as a whole begins to develop humility for learning, empathy, courage for facing losses, and discernment for naming and navigating competing values. As they begin to experiment, to face failures, and to develop resilience in the face of the resistance, they "spend down" the trust that they have earned to hold onto those who will pull back when the losses mount up, the failures pile up, the uncertainty increases, and the learning hasn't yet caught up to the reality of the moment.

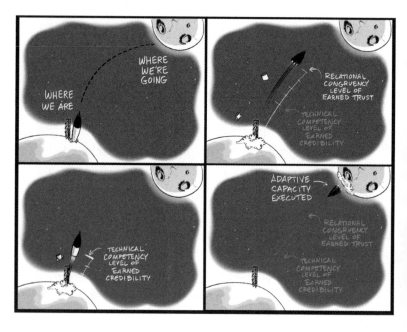

So how does a leader help a team stay focused on this most difficult assignment? How does she take the organization through the process of transformation without losing all of the trust needed to "stay alive"? Through, in the words of Marty Linsky, "disappointing your own people *at a rate they can absorb.*"

"At a rate they can absorb."

Change leaders need a process that will enable them to engage people in their own transformation at the right pace and without wasting the time or opportunity necessary for the transformation to occur. *The old mindset of storing up trust must give way to a new adaptive reset of investing trust in transformation.*

This reset is developed through a new skillset:

1. Creating a holding environment (Your people can trust that the transformation is being shaped by the genuine work of discernment held by a trustworthy team.)

2. Clarifying your charism (Your people can trust that even as they prepare to change, what is most precious and important about the organization will be preserved.)

3. Paying attention to pain points (Your people can trust that the necessary changes are going to make a real difference in the world.)

BALCONY
SESSION

1 WHAT IS YOUR FIRST
RESPONSE to the DEFINITION of
LEADERSHIP as "DISAPPOINTING
YOUR OWN PEOPLE at a RATE
THEY CAN ABSORB"? HOW HAVE
YOU EXPERIENCED or LIVED OUT
that DEFINITION EITHER as a
LEADER or ONE WORKING WITH a
LEADER?

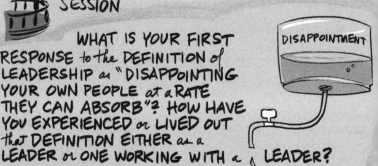

DISAPPOINTMENT

2 THINK BACK on YOUR LIFE
WORKING WITH DIFFERENT
LEADERS. WHO IS the MOST
TRUSTWORTHY LEADER YOU
KNOW? WHAT is it ABOUT THEM
that MADE THEM TRUSTWORTHY?

3 IF THAT TRUSTWORTHY
LEADER WAS GOING to MAKE
CHANGES that WOULD be
PERSONALLY PAINFUL for YOU
or DIFFICULT for YOU to ADJUST
to, WHAT WOULD YOU NEED
FROM HIM or HER?

EMPATHY
TRUTH
WARNING
TRANSITION
COMPENSATION
OPTIONS

TRAINING
GUIDANCE
HELP
PATHWAY
CLARITY
CONNECTION

ALTERNATIVES
RECOGNITION
ASSISTANCE
LOVE
PACKAGE

CHAPTER 3
NEW SKILLSET PART 1:
CREATE A HOLDING ENVIRONMENT

Hal was a man who had lost his sight. Gus was confined to a wheelchair following an amputation. Alone, they would each be people who are sometimes called "shut-ins." Octogenarians both when I was their pastor, they didn't get around very easily on their own. When they used to attend worship services at our church, Hal would push Gus and Gus would direct Hal. They would make their way through the parking lot and the patio to their place together in the pew. Gus would sit in his wheelchair and give direction; Hal would push the wheelchair and follow Gus's lead. Together they would get to where they wanted to go. A blind man who can't see, giving energy to a man who can't walk. A man who can't move, giving direction to a man who lacks vision.[1]

Whenever I think of them, I smile. Two friends who genuinely trust each other work together in a way that enables each of them to go where they couldn't alone. This is what leadership looks like in a world where most of us really can't see what's ahead or where we may not have the skills or stamina to move ahead: we are all Gus and Hal going together.

> True transformation is always
> bigger than anything that any
> one leader can accomplish.

NO *ONE* CAN BRING TRANSFORMATION

An individual leader with enough trust and authority can stop dysfunction and evil. She can get laws changed and policies adopted. He can use his authority to hire and fire to change the players. One leader can remake meetings, set agendas, and attend to the problems that everyone agrees needs to be done. But true transformation is not a change in agendas or policies or meetings or org charts. True transformation is a change of heart, a shift in values or attitudes or behaviors. *And this transformation requires that the people themselves change themselves.* As Heifetz and Linsky put it, "The sustainability of change depends on having the people with the problem internalize the change itself."[2]

To do this, transformational leaders cannot rely on their own charisma and credibility alone. They have to bring people together and hold people together for the work of change. In

an address to a Duke Divinity School Convocation, Ronald Heifetz said, "Adaptive processes don't require leadership with answers. It requires leadership that *creates structures that hold people together* through the very conflictive, passionate, and sometimes awful process of addressing questions for which there aren't easy answers."[3]

This is the thinking behind the first skillset: *creating a team of people who become the container for holding the trust invested in transformation.* Heifetz, Linsky, and their colleagues refer to this as a "holding environment."[4] While they use the word "structures," what they really mean is far more an expression of *relationships* than a formal configuration of policies, procedures, and rules. "A holding environment consists of all those ties that bind people together and enable them to maintain their collective focus on what they are trying to do. All the human sources of cohesion."[5]

> Transformational leaders must
> bring people together and hold people
> together for the work of change.

DUTCH-OVEN LEADERSHIP

Imagine that you are cooking a big meal for a big, hungry family. You decide to make a stew in a big cast-iron Dutch oven.[6] You get raw meat, hard vegetables, some stock, and seasoning. You put them in the Dutch oven and with enough time at the right temperature, you get a feast. You have to tend to it, yes. And without question the Dutch oven can burn you if you are not careful, but if you can maintain the right temperature for the right amount of time, keep stirring it so that things don't stick and burn, and don't get too impatient and crank it up, you'll have success.

This takes attention. If the temperature gets too high, the meal gets burned; too low and even though a long time may have gone by, all you will have is hard vegetables and raw meat. Indeed, if you leave the food in the pot without enough heat, it will eventually spoil before it turns into a meal. Regulating the fire and keeping the *right* amount of heat is critical. But so is having a good, big pot that can hold the food and the heat for as long as needed for the "transformation" of meat and vegetables into a delicious dinner.

Bringing good, healthy change to any organization is like cooking a stew in a Dutch oven. Every person—all with their own identities, opinions, and beliefs—is a like a hard, raw vegetable or a firm piece of uncooked meat. For the pieces of food to become a meal that will feed a hungry tribe, each bit must be transformed at least a bit. The Dutch oven is the holding environment—*the relationships of the group* that will take on the heat of change. In a holding environment, the leader's job is to regulate the heat so that transformation can occur. When we are all so comfortable that we are complacent, we don't want to go anywhere. When we are camped under a tree in the shade, even staying in the wilderness seems better than heading off for the

Promised Land. But when the heat of urgency and opportunity, of appropriate anxiety and crisis of changing conditions gets turned up thoughtfully and insightfully—*and held well by the trusting relationships of a good team*—we begin to move toward the land of milk and honey that we really long for.

> In a holding environment,
> the leader's job is to regulate the heat
> so that transformation can occur.

A STRONG HOLDING ENVIRONMENT REQUIRES A TEAM OF TEAMS

When United States Army General Stanley McChrystal was assigned to lead the Joint Special Operations Task Force during the war in Iraq in 2003, he brought with him all of the expertise, experience, and credibility of years of the best military training. But he soon discovered, in his own words,

> although lavishly resourced and exquisitely trained, we found ourselves losing to an enemy that, by traditional

calculus, we should have dominated. Over time we came to realize that more than our foe, we were actually struggling to cope with an environment that was fundamentally different from anything we'd planned or trained for.[7]

For McChrystal, this disrupted environment, marked by continuous change and uncertainty, led him to eventually recognize that the entire "command and control" approach that had been the cornerstone of military strategy and philosophy was the problem. Instead of a rigid division of responsibilities and unquestioned commitment to a strategy that was planned in a conference room a world away, they required a new way of operating on a large scale. "Almost everything we did ran against the grain of military tradition and of general organizational practice," McChrystal wrote. They needed to be a holding environment, or what McChrystal calls a "team of teams."[8]

Every architect needs both a bank to fund the project and a construction team to build it. Every visionary leader needs both a group to keep attending to the necessary work and a team to lead the transformation of the organizational culture. And while they may be one and the same in some circumstances, a great idea often needs at least *two* teams to see it through: the *maintaining mission group* and the *transformation team*.[9]

The maintaining mission group has to be committed to giving safety, time, space, protection, and resources to the project. At first, members of this group don't need to actually do anything except *not* create obstacles and not sabotage the change process (a big task, in itself!). At best, they actively voice support, they keep a steady hand at the wheel, and they monitor the inevitable anxiety. They provide cover for the transformation team while also caring for the organization. They make sure that the community feels safe while a few are venturing forth. They reassure stakeholders that while change may be needed, there is a group of people committed to the ongoing health and preservation of all that is most important about the shared mission.

In most organizational settings, this is work of a board of directors. They don't so much have to make it happen as buy-in *enough* to give the transformation team *time to make it happen*. They have to understand and own the changes, but not necessarily give much personal energy to them. Or to shift the metaphor, they need to keep the wagon train moving even while the scouts ahead are looking for a new pass through the mountains.

Eventually, this group is the most important. This is the group that will choose to institutionalize the change or not. This team protects the culture

of the organization, and it is the team that can single-handedly thwart the transformation if they choose to do so.

BUILDING A TRULY TRANSFORMATIVE TEAM

Recruiting and selecting a transformation team is one of the most important aspects of leading change. This is the group of people who are going to experiment their way forward. They are going to do the work of listening, learning, attempting, and, yes, failing. This team needs to be innovative and persistent, cohesive and communicative. In many situations, this could be a designated staff team, but often it is not. Indeed, in nonprofit settings, it is usually a mistake to assume that the staff is going to be the transformation team. In churches, for example, the transformation teams need to be made up of both staff and lay leaders. In any organization, the transformation team requires both those who have authoritative positions and those with informal influence. The transformation team must reflect the diversity of the organization and be made up of people who are dedicated to the whole organization and not just one constituency, who are ready to take on the challenges of a changing environment.[10]

Give the work back to the people who most care about it. If "adaptive leadership is *the practice of mobilizing people* to tackle tough challenges and thrive," then if nobody is being mobilized, nobody is being led.[11] This is a critical moment in organizational transformation. While we absolutely need people to keep raising awareness of what is not working in our midst, we must remember that nothing really changes by complaining. Only when someone steps up to convene a group to address a problem does transformation occur. When a group of people bring a complaint,

don't jump to fix it, but instead engage those who raised the complaint in the process of transformation. Find the people who are most feeling the pain of the challenge, and recruit and invite them to take it on with you.

Engage the mature and motivated. Let's face it, most of the work of leading an organization is putting out fires, dealing with the resistant, attending to the cranky, and trying to appease the complainers. These tasks are part of our work, and indeed, we are called to these people as well. But when it is time to lead on, more and more of your energy must be invested in those who are motivated to grow and take

responsibility for themselves. So, learning to recognize, invest in, and work with the mature and motivated is a huge advantage.

A true transformation team is more about the energy and engagement that someone brings to the challenge than the members' status or place in the organizational chart. They are the very ones who are going to experience the organizational changes first. Long before anyone else is going to see the changes that are being made, the transformation team is going to be in the middle of them. They will see the challenges of the future before anyone else; they will have to face the losses and own up to their own resistance before bringing others along.

Michaela O'Donnell, executive director of the DePree Center for Leadership, models for us the kind of character needed in holding environments:

> My approach to leading change is focus on what first needs to change . . . about me. I start with that every time. When resistance comes externally, I have come to pay attention to the resistance within me. When I do so, it builds trust with others. People see that I am doing the same thing I am asking them to do.[12]

Increase the number and volume of diverse voices at the table. For a team to be truly trustworthy and have the capacity to see the future, it must be made up of a combination of experienced stakeholders who have influence and authority in the organization *and* emerging or often-neglected leaders who can bring a different perspective. Numerous studies have demonstrated that the most moral, effective, and enduring leadership teams are the most diverse. Adaptive leadership is built on the biological reality that the capacity to thrive in a changing environment is linked to creating a system with the most diversity possible. And adaptive changes that move beyond technical solutions very often need the diversity of perspectives from people who have not been the experts of the past. In the words of innovative change leader Dave Gibbons, "The future is here, it is just on the margins."[13]

In short, the transformation team must be comprised of the most diverse, creative, energetic, mature, and motivated people in the organization. They must be
both enthusiastic for
the idea, resolute

about seeing it through, and willing to expend relational capital to bring genuine culture change. Perhaps most im-portant, eventually, they also need to be prepared—when the time is right—to disband and give their influence back to the authorized leaders of the maintaining the mission group so that the organization itself will embrace and institutionalize the changes.

It takes *two* teams to create a trustworthy holding environment—who must start by taking a long look back before moving forward.

BALCONY SESSION

1. WHAT is the BEST TEAM that YOU HAVE EVER BEEN ON? (ANY KIND of TEAM: SPORTS? WORKING GROUP? CRISIS RESPONSE?) WHAT MADE IT SO GOOD?

2. MAKE a LIST of the PEOPLE in YOUR ORGANIZATION WHOSE NAMES or FACES CAME to MIND as YOU READ ABOUT the QUALITIES NEEDED for CREATING a GOOD HOLDING ENVIRONMENT. WHAT WOULD YOU NEED to RE-ARRANGE in YOUR OWN LIFE to START BUILDING a "TEAM of TEAMS" that CAN HOLD BOTH the TRUST & the TRANSFORMATION of YOUR ORGANIZATION?

TRUST   CHANGE

H
L

3. WHEN YOU CONSIDER the QUALITIES NEEDED to "REGULATE the HEAT" of a HOLDING ENVIRONMENT, WHAT WILL it REQUIRE of YOUR OWN LEADERSHIP?

CHAPTER 4
NEW SKILLSET PART 2: CLARIFY YOUR CHARISM

It's not "human genius"

that makes us human, but an old love,

an old intelligence of the heart

we gather to us from the world,

from the creatures, from the angels

of inspiration, from the dead—

an intelligence merely nonexistent

to those who do not have it, but

to those who have it more dear than life.[1]

These lines from poet Wendell Berry capture perfectly why I appreciate adaptive leadership: it is about the thriving of an organization as a living *organism*, a body, as it were. This organizational body has purpose that has been cultivated by people who have given themselves to it with energy, imagination, sacrifice, courage, even love. This community, institution, company, or church has both a life and a history;

it is made up of more than policies and procedures but has been crafted by people with deep care. This is why the leaders must function as a high-trust holding environment, and this is why we don't start a change process by running headlong into the challenges that require change.

Because leaders are dealing with something living and precious to people, adaptive leadership insists that when an organism-like organization is facing a disrupted or changing environment, the two teams of "holding environment" leaders must themselves "hold" *two* commitments simultaneously:[2]

1. Maintaining our *charism*, that is, the gift of our values and identity that comes from the history and identity that makes each organization unique.

2. Wisely adapting or being transformed in order for the organization to thrive and for the gift to continue to serve the larger world at a point of pain.[3]

This "dual conviction" means that when starting to lead a change process, we don't actually start with what needs to change, but what should *not* change. So, the place to start when moving forward into the future is with a long, loving look back into our past—with identifying our values and clarifying what has been our historical charism. Indeed, to paraphrase two respected leadership scholars, before we

change anything, we must first spend time and energy to get clear on what should *never* change.[4]

This is difficult for many enthusiastic change leaders to do. Everything with us is energized by moving ahead, exploring what is around the next corner, "skating to where the puck is going" (as hockey great Wayne Gretzky used to say).[5] To slow down and focus on what is so valuable that it needs to be preserved feels like we are intentionally pumping the brakes right when everything within us wants to push the accelerator to the floor.

> Before we change anything, we need to
> get clear on what should never change.

Further, most leaders impatiently tell me, "We don't need to look back; we are ready to go forward! We already know our values! We have a list of values. We went to great lengths to create values that we should adhere to in all that we do!"

When I affirm them and ask them to explain how they came to those values, it usually sounds something like this:

So the leadership team gathered for a two-day offsite. We spent a lot of time talking and dreaming and we asked ourselves, "What should our values be? What should we be about? What should we make sure that we tell everyone in our organization matters most?"

We read books, we thought hard about it, we made long lists, and had passionate conversations. Then we reduced the list down to five values and we turned them into a mnemonic that was easily remembered: GRACE. We believe we should always be Generous, Reconciling, Accountable, Committed, Excellent.

These are our values. We have printed them up and put them on the walls of the office so that everyone can see them. We may not always live them out, but this is what we believe we should be.

And that is where I gently stop them. *That is really inspiring. But your values aren't your values,* I tell them. When their brows furrow and they begin to protest, I continue.

Do you know how I know that? Because you kept repeating one word: should. Should is aspirational. Should is filled with conviction about what we ought to do. This inspiring acronym of words is not representative of your actual values; they are your aspirations. They are beautiful and convicting, and certainly important and even valuable to at least a small group of people. But they aren't your actual values, they are your aspirational values. They are what the leadership team thinks you should be.

Your actual values are revealed in what you actually do. Values are what is already true about you and are based on what you have done or are already doing. Your actual values are no less inspiring, but they are not hopes for what you could be, but expressions of who you actually are.

Who you actually are is the starting point for the transformation into who you need to become. And that starting point does not come with dreams for the future or aspirations for what

we should be, but by looking back at who you have always been at your best and most inspiring.

> Who you actually are is the starting
> point for the transformation into
> who you need to become.

Our actual values keep us focused on becoming who we are and not trying to be something we will never be. We don't want to be like a liturgical church trying to reach younger people by changing their name from St. Bartholomew Episcopal to "The Flood," exchanging vestments for skinny jeans, and transforming the sanctuary into a soundstage with a kicking band and a smoke machine.

In adaptive change, each organization is understood to be a "body" with particular and unique traits that must be honored in any change process. Our actual values remind us of what has actually been valuable to ourselves and to others. They help us describe our identity and our uniqueness. They are "the DNA" of the organization.

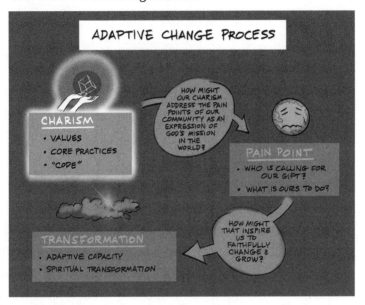

FROM CORE VALUES TO CHARISM

The shared values that make up the DNA of an organization, what Brafman and Beckstrom, authors of *The Starfish and the Spider*, call "ideology," are what give the organization life. If shared values are not "protected and passed down," then the organization ceases to be. Indeed, as Brafman and Beckstrom write, "Values *are* the organization."[6]

In biology, DNA "contains the genetic information that allows all modern living things to function, grow and reproduce."[7] In human bodies, our DNA is a "code" that makes each of us unique, helps us to survive and thrive, and it is what we pass on to offspring in reproduction. In organizational systems thinking, the "DNA" of a group is a way of describing the essential and unique attributes—the "defining essence" or "code"—of that group.[8] Every organization has a history, a set of core values and beliefs, a cultural and shared DNA, an organizational "code."

> The "DNA" of a group is a way of
> describing the essential and unique
> attributes—the "defining essence"
> or "code"—of that group.

In our work with faith-based organizations, we coach leaders to understand that since transformation always requires facing the losses of letting go of some of the most cherished values, behaviors, and attitudes of the past, we must first prove ourselves trustworthy in protecting the core of beliefs that gives an organization its identity. In order to earn the credibility to lead people into what can be—and what they will need to face and potentially let go of to become what can be—we have to demonstrate fidelity to what is. In a presentation to Duke Divinity School in 2008, Ronald Heifetz put it this way:

Most real change is not about change. It's about identifying what cultural DNA is worth conserving, is precious and essential, and that indeed *makes it worth suffering the losses* so that you can find a way to bring the best of your tradition and history and values into the future.[9]

"TELL ME A STORY"

Because for change to last it must be a *healthy adaptation of core organizational DNA*, the first exercise we offer clients helps them *uncover the actual values*—the DNA—of their organization.[10] We call this "Tell Me a Story" (TMAS). TMAS is a simple experience that asks stakeholders in the organization to gather in small, informal, comfortable groups and just tell stories from the history of the organization. This can be done around tables in a larger gathering or over a meal in smaller settings. The only requirement is that the groups themselves be as diverse as possible (different ages, different backgrounds or socioeconomic status, different levels of involvement in the organization, different tenures of involvement) so as to represent the whole organization as much as possible.

We ask all of them to take a moment and think of a story they would tell from the organization's history that is most meaningful to them. *What story of our organization causes a lump in your throat or comes from the heart?*

"Tell me a story," we say, about . . .

→ A hero in the organization's history who you wish everybody could have known . . .

→ A moment when you were most proud to be part of this organization . . .

→ An event or occasion that made you say, "We are not perfect, but *this* is what we are really all about . . ."

→ A decision made by leadership that made you say, "This is why I am here . . ."

→ A crisis or opportunity that was handled in such a way that you thought, "This is when I knew I had found my people . . ."

We encourage each person to think about it for a bit and let one compelling story come to mind. Then with as much time as it takes to tell them, let each person tell the story to the group. If different people end up telling the same story or mentioning the same event or the same hero, *it is a good thing*. Like the way a family tells the same story over and over again, hearing multiple stories that reinforce the same history is one of the ways that we celebrate our shared experiences and shared commitments. The goal isn't to be exhaustive, but intensive—underlining what is most cherished about our organizational history.

> For change to last it must be a *healthy* adaptation of core organizational DNA.

When the stories are being told, don't take notes. Don't analyze or dissect the stories. Just listen to them together. Celebrate them. Enjoy them. Pay attention to what makes people feel deeply. Linger when there are tears, take in the shared laughter and old jokes. Let healthy nostalgia and common history remind us of what we love and why we are the kinds of people who have been so committed to this organization, its work, and its people.

Remember that it doesn't matter how long each person has been engaged in the organization. It doesn't matter what role they have played or how invested they have been. Everyone speaks into the storytelling from their own perspective, whatever it is.

When the stories have finished, we encourage a little break. If this was done over a meal, this would be a good time to clear the table, put on a pot of coffee, and bring out a bit of dessert.

Then when reconvened, the group answers some questions. A convener or moderator would start taking notes now, capturing these responses for later:

→ Which stories were most powerful or most often repeated?

→ What are the values displayed *in those most powerful or repeated stories*?

→ Of all the values that we could preserve, what are—*from the stories*—most important?

→ Identify three to five values and write them down.

Notice that the emphasis of the discussion is to focus on the stories and the values revealed. Brené Brown says that stories are "data with a soul."[11] The stories give us actual "data" about what we have historically valued—and even currently really value. In this moment, the group has to resist the desire to make the data say what they *want* it to say by imposing values on the stories, but honestly and collaboratively mine the stories for the actual values.

Those actual values are deeply important. To be sure, *not every actual value is positive and worthy of preserving* (organizational values based on some of the deep systemic sins of the past immediately come to mind). But being able to name them out loud, articulate with some degree of understanding what these values meant at one time, and then discern how to adapt and even—when necessary, discard—a historic but problematic value builds trust with those who see themselves as preservers of the organization's history and legacy, and with those who are most eager for change. Those values also help leaders get clear on what is unique and even most valuable about the organization and—with some wise discernment—will help clarify the organizational "charism."

WHAT MAKES YOU *YOU*?

What is most unique about your organization?

What is your organization's unique contribution—or value that it adds—to your community or your world?

What is, that is to say, your *charism*?

Charism is the description of how a group's core values are most repeatedly and naturally embodied in a way that benefits others. It is what is both universal and unique about an organization. Charism is what makes the organization more than just a group of friends or a club. The concept of charism comes from Catholic orders. It expresses the unique historical strength of the order that was inspired by the "gifts" of the founder for building up the church, as well as "*a specific intent* in the community and the world."[12] So, while all Catholic orders hold to the same core beliefs and share similar practices for their religious life, their charism describes their missional value to the world.

> What is our organization's unique contribution—or value that we add— to our community or our world?

For example, compare the difference between the Benedictine retreat center near my home in Los Angeles and a Jesuit University anywhere around the world. Both were established by Catholic orders founded by a saint, both would hold masses and teach the Catholic faith, both are led by and supported by Catholic priests and lay leaders who hold to a common set of doctrines and beliefs.

The Benedictine retreat center focuses its work on the integration of work and prayer, deeply rooted in a spirituality that "attunes us to an awareness of the divine in the ordinary."[13] A person coming on a retreat at a Benedictine center would likely be greeted warmly, shown to a simple room, and immediately invited for prayer. They don't ask if you are Catholic or even if you are Christian; you are just invited to join with the regular community prayers. And if you stay more than a few days, you just might be invited to do some dishes. For Benedictines, the "gift" that they offer the world is to show how God is present in the routines of everyday life, as available to you when you are standing at a sink as when you are kneeling in a sanctuary.

Jesuits have historically been the "soldiers" of the Catholic church, the missionaries who will go anywhere in the world "for the greater glory of God." Their sixteenth-century founder Ignatius of Loyola believed that the ideal Jesuit "lived with one foot raised," always looking to respond to emerging opportunities to "help souls."[14] Their charism has been marked by flexibility, creativity, and a willingness to be sent anywhere there is a need.

So, while the Benedictine charism led them to found monasteries teaching rhythms of prayer and work, the Jesuits founded universities and social movements for engaging different social and spiritual challenges in the world. While the Benedictines are committed to specific locations and living in community together, the Jesuits are trained in spiritual exercises that are "portable" and can be utilized in any setting the Jesuit may find himself serving God.

Gordon T. Smith, president of Ambrose University in Calgary in Alberta, Canada, explained charism in an interview:

> Charism provides a way to talk about who we are in light of something bigger than ourselves and unique to ourselves. It allows us to differentiate ourselves from other institutions while also valuing the other institution. It helps us see that our gift and vocation is different from that of our sister institutions (and sometimes competitors!) and enables us to pray for them, support them, and collaborate with them.[15]

Charism allows leaders to frame the change as an expression of identity and reframe it to motivate others for expressing that identity in a changing world. It is often a reiteration of the original purpose of the founders. It is usually rediscovered in unpacking the stories of how that

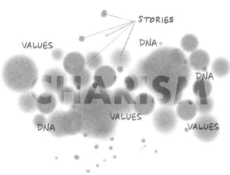

STORIES REVEAL OUR CHARISM

original DNA continues to show up in the organization at critical moments, reminding members of its original calling. When an organization examines its charism, there should be a sense of recognition (this is us!) and a gentle sense of repentance (this is where we may have strayed from who we are). To return and rediscover the organizational charism is to renew the healthiest part of the original purpose with the conviction that if the "spirit" of the original mission still resounds today, the charism is then adapted for the particular context and challenges of the day.

MINDING THE GAP

The storytelling exercise and the identification of actual values is both a tender and sometimes slightly unsettling experience for the group. While telling stories and affirming the actual values of an organization through capturing the best parts of the organizational DNA is affirming, there will always be some values that are not identified. The stories/data reveal the difference between what we say we value and what we have actually valued.

So when we say we are an organization that values all generations but there are no stories about young people . . .

Or we say we are a school that is devoted to excellence in teaching but most of our stories are about our research, publications, and awards (and less about students) . . .

Or we say we are a company that values having a balanced and healthy life and all the stories are about heroes who overworked, sacrificed their health and well-being (and sometimes even their families) for the company . . .

We find the gaps between our actual and aspirational DNA.

And in this gap, we begin to identify the work that needs to be done to move from trust to transformation—to shift values, attitudes, or behaviors in a healthy way that furthers our mission today.

Do we know which values, attitudes, and behaviors need to be preserved?

Do we know which values, attitudes, and behaviors need to be adapted or discarded?

And what helps us decide?

To get clearer on that, we need to go outside.

BALCONY SESSION

1 WHICH of YOUR CURRENT ORGANIZATIONAL VALUES WOULD YOU EXPECT to be REVEALED MORE as ASPIRATIONS than ACTUAL VALUES?

2 HOW EASILY CAN YOU CONNECT YOUR CURRENT VALUES to a STORY FROM the PAST that is REPEATED OVER & OVER AGAIN, EMOTIONALLY LADEN, & CHERISHED WITHIN YOUR ORGANIZATIONAL CULTURE?

3 USING ONLY YOUR ACTUAL VALUES as the "DATA" HOW WOULD YOU DESCRIBE the CHARISM of YOUR ORGANIZATION — the UNIQUE GIFT that it OFFERS the WORLD?

CHAPTER 5
NEW SKILLSET PART 3:
PAY ATTENTION TO PAIN POINTS

"Tod, look, there is only really one thing that matters if you are going to try to lead something innovative: Does it fix a real problem? Can you tell us what pain point in the world or the church your school's new project would be trying to address?"

I still feel sheepish looking back on it now, but I had spent the morning in a Silicon Valley conference room with a group of venture capitalists, entrepreneurs, and executives in the innovative tech space. They had gathered at the request of a board member of the institution that I was serving and another friend who asked them if they would give a few hours to offer feedback on a new initiative I was leading.

After giving a ten-minute presentation on the need for the changes that I was suggesting so that the organization would survive, these Silicon Valley leaders gently corrected my glaring shortsightedness. *Nobody cares if your institution survives*, they said to me, *they only care if your institution cares about them.* Any truly transformational strategy must be focused on the needs of real people in the real world. At that moment the conversation with the Silicon Valley venture capitalists pivoted from what the organization wanted me to do to what the world needed to have done.

Just when I was about to crawl under the table in embarrassment at my blind spot, a venture capitalist in the room said, "Isn't this what Jesus was all about? Didn't he teach us that one of the most important things is to focus on *loving our neighbors* as much as ourselves?" Whenever the venture capitalist has to remind the guy with the theology degrees about something so fundamental to the faith, it's clearly not a good day for the theologian.

Groups, however—even Christian groups—are hardwired to default to their own survival. Because we are doing something as an expression of our faith, it becomes easy to assume organizational survival at any cost is pleasing to God. After a while a Christian mission can be little more than keeping a Christian organization or church alive. (I often have to remind church leaders that *none* of Paul's churches are alive today—but the faith that we share certainly is.)

Even more to the point, most of us unconsciously believe that survival usually means reinforcing the way the way we have done things that worked in the past. So, when an organization feels stress, the default behavior of most organizational leaders is to solve the problems *for our organizations* rather than *change our organizations for meeting the needs of the world*. The result is that instead of undergoing transformation to be more effective in our mission to serve the world, organizations unconsciously reinforce the very status quo that is no longer working.[1]

> Nobody cares if your institution
> survives, they only care if your
> institution cares about them.

Leadership, as my Silicon Valley counselors were reminding me, is called into action when there is a problem or condition coming from *outside* of the organization that needs to be addressed with changes *inside* the organization. It is focused on helping the organization change in order to take on that challenge. This flies in the face of so much leadership writing that insists that change begins in an awe-inspiring vision given by a charismatic and compelling leader assuring us that better days are ahead—for us!

For Jim Collins, leading change does not begin in a stirring vision but in a disciplined process of "confronting the brutal facts." For Collins, much like the Silicon Valley leaders who challenged my inward, institutionally focused approach to innovation, the genesis of change is *not our inspired ideas but the pain, problems, brokenness, and challenges we see in the world*. Change leaders don't arise from a great vision, they are raised to meet a great need.[2]

One of the genuine crises of so much leadership—even faith leadership—today is how inwardly focused it is. Leaders quickly become consumed with helping a company, a congregation, an organization, or an educational institution survive. It's not enough to turn around a declining organization, resolve conflict, restore a sense of community, regain a business's market share, return an organization to sustainability, or even "save the company." The real question before any leader of an organization is "save the company *for what*?"[3]

> The real question before any leader of an organization is "save the company *for what*?"

In 2023 and 2024, my company worked with the President's Council and Strategic Planning Group of Baylor University to create a strategic plan for the next season of Baylor's mission as a university. Fresh off a tremendously successful season where they had restored the trust of the "Baylor Family" (as they affectionately call it) after a sexual abuse scandal, Baylor had become one of the most respected schools in the country after weathering the Covid-19 crisis, had raised over $1 billion, and had achieved Research-1 status (the highest classification) as an elite research university three years earlier than expected. After becoming the only school in that R1 category with an "explicit and primary identity as a Protestant faith-based institution," you could forgive them for wanting to rest on their laurels for a bit.[4] They certainly had survived. Yet if survival was the only goal, they would not have engaged my company to start a new strategic planning process.

But President Linda Livingstone insisted that with one strategic plan for restoring trust finished, it was time to consider what they could do to make a difference for good in the world. When she was inaugurated as president in 2017 in the wake of the scandal, Livingstone had declared, "The world needs a Baylor": "The world needs a Baylor that raises the bar in the area of Christian higher education, combining the riches of undergraduate, professional and graduate education with rigorous research, high-quality athletics and unwavering faith commitment."[5]

In 2023, having accomplished the task of restoring trust, President Livingstone and her executive team now pressed itself to consider how the charism of Baylor as an unambiguously Christian and academically elite institution could make a greater impact in the world. In short, the question of the next strategic plan would be, "The world needs a Baylor . . . *for what*?"

When we work with organizations, after they have done the work of listening to their most committed "stakeholders" and clarifying the actual values and charism of the organization, we then ask them to spend a considerable amount of time listening *outside* of the institution.

We ask every member of the transformation team (the group that is working with us on the actual change initiative—which I will discuss in more detail later), to conduct three to five interviews with people in their lives who are *outside* the organization. These are not surveys but conversations. They don't have to knock on doors or accost strangers; they are supposed to talk to people in their lives, people they are comfortable talking with and whose opinions genuinely interest them.

The one rule is that they cannot be members of the organization. If this is a church, then no church members; a nonprofit work, then no donors or participants or beneficiaries. If it is a college or university, then no student, faculty, staff, or alums. If it is a company, then no employees or customers. The goal is to get an outside perspective of someone talking to you from your own life.

They ask people in their networks three simple questions about the community that they live in:

1. What makes it good to live in a place like this?

2. What sometimes makes it hard to live in a place like this?

3. If good people came together to do what they could together to make it good for everyone to live in a place like this, what would you most want them to do?

And that's it. Sometimes we adapt the questions to focus on the particular constituents that an organization serves, but they are always focused around three external themes: What is good? What is not so good? And what could make it better for everyone? They ask the questions, they write  down the answers, and they bring them back to the group for shared learning. Notice that they don't ask *any* questions about the church, organization, company, or institution. This is not a "customer satisfaction survey" but a genuine conversation among neighbors and friends about their hopes and longings for the world and their community. These questions help the change leadership team get their focus off their own internal concerns of surviving and solving institutional questions, and instead encourage them to listen deeply for a renewed sense of calling and purpose.

To answer their "for what" question, Baylor's Strategic Planning Group not only conducted nearly one hundred focus groups of their faculty, staff, students, and community leaders—and sent surveys to their forty thousand members of the Baylor Family— but also conducted interviews with dozens of people from *outside* the institution to ask the deeper question about what Baylor, with its resources, values, and commitments, could do.

We then led the Strategic Planning Group through a process of discernment around questions of organizational calling or vocation:

➜ What pain in the world is calling for our charism?

➜ Based on what we are most gifted for, what is ours to do?

That process of discernment became the central question for the next season of Baylor's mission as a university, and that same process and question must be the central point of discernment for any organization.

Then with both the charism clarified and the pain point placed right in front of us, we turn to a more difficult question—the question that most of us resist. *How might that inspire us to faithfully change and grow?*

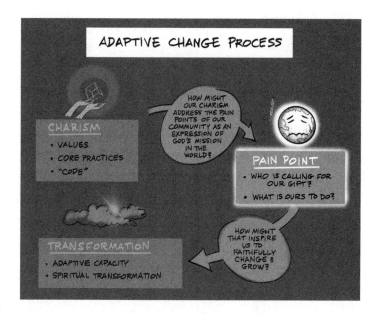

Pause and consider these questions in light of the changing world that you are facing and the challenges that it puts before you:

→ What is our charism?

→ What pain point in the world is calling for our charism?

→ What deep change is needed for us to live out that calling?

This is the transformation and the truly adaptive challenge: *investing in the deep change needed for the organization to live out its calling, its mission—the work that is theirs to do in attending to the pain points of the world.*

BALCONY SESSION

1. TAKE a MOMENT to FOCUS on a QUESTION INSPIRED by ONE that the SILICON VALLEY TECH LEADERS ASKED ME: WHAT WAS the REAL PROBLEM in the WORLD that OUR ORGANIZATION WAS FOUNDED to ADDRESS?

2. WHAT INPUT COULD YOU GET FROM PEOPLE OUTSIDE YOUR ORGANIZATION to GET a BETTER SENSE of HOW YOUR ORGANIZATIONAL CHARISM COULD PAY MORE ATTENTION to a REAL PAIN POINT in the WORLD?

3. HOW MIGHT the PAIN POINTS of the WORLD TODAY REQUIRE US to REFOCUS OUR STRATEGY, EFFORTS, & INTERNAL STRUCTURES?

CHAPTER 6
ADAPTIVE RESET:
INVEST TRUST IN TRANSFORMATION

In the Gospel of Luke, Jesus tells the story of a rich man who stored up so much wealth that he had to keep building bigger barns to hold all of his "grain and goods." The story comes in the midst of a longer set of messages that Jesus spoke to people who were fearful and worrying. Instead of Jesus' customary compassion and reassurance that they had nothing to fear and worry about, this particular story ends with the rich man with the big barns being told that his storehouses had been a massive waste of time. For that night, he was told, was his last (Lk 12:13-21).

It's as if even Jesus couldn't stomach the idea that those who had so much of anything good would hoard it for themselves instead of using it to make other people's lives a little bit better.

In many ways, this is the biggest challenge of this little book.

So, you are a leader that people trust? You have the skills and the character, the technical competence and relational congruence that make people look to you as a leader? You are safe and secure up on your pedestal, and people listen to your voice and honor your perspective?

Good for you.

So . . . *what are you going to do with all of that?*

The adaptive reset for leadership in a changing world is that while trust is an invaluable resource for change, it is also just a resource. Trustworthy leadership is ultimately not for stockpiling for the leader's security, but for having a resource to invest in what really makes a difference—transformation.

> It's as if even Jesus couldn't stomach the idea that those who had so much of anything good would hoard it for themselves instead of using it to make other people's lives a little bit better.

Adaptive challenges, the most demanding set of problems that are beyond our old best practices—if they are to be faced—require the transformation of a group of people. They necessitate the whole organization not only embracing the challenge but personally experiencing the change. And that is never easy.

→ A corporation like IBM retools to serve "international" (I) "businesses" (B)—no longer with "machines" (M), but in corporate consulting.

→ A nonprofit organization realizes that its funding model of relying on large donors with institutional loyalty must adjust to engage a younger generation energized by particular causes.

→ A university shifts from residential to online education in order to express a value of making education accessible to more people.

→ A community begins to name the implicit biases that have lingered unspoken from its history in the years of racial segregation.

→ A mission agency shifts from sending workers from the Majority World to empowering and resourcing local workers.

→ A church faces the reality that its aging congregation is unable to keep a younger generation that is walking away from the faith.

Changes like these necessitate a group of people to be transformed in some deep, uncomfortable, and often reorienting ways. They require a shift in values, attitudes, or behaviors to both see and then solve the challenge. This is, to be sure, the difference between technical change and adaptive change. As Jim Osterhaus and his colleagues have written, "Technical change is change on the surface, using strategies and knowledge familiar to us. Sometimes technical change is good and even necessary, but it is not deep change. Adaptive change is deep change on the level of values, beliefs, and behavior."[1]

And that is always a risk. Deep, disruptive transformation is going to cost everyone. It will cost the stakeholders of an organization their peace of mind, their complacency, and their comfort. When you start asking people to face losses and give things up for the sake of a bigger mission, the cheers and bouquets and tributes begin to vanish. It will cost leaders a good deal of that trust that they have stored away in the big barns.

> **Adaptive challenges, the most demanding set of problems that are beyond our old best practices—if they are to be faced—require the transformation of a group of people.**

Transformative leaders then realize that they must learn to *invest trust in transformation and learn to refill the trust accounts so that they can be invested again*.

Transformation requires a costly *investment of* and *reinvestment in* trust. To do so well and in a way that preserves and even restores trust throughout the change process means to utilize a "team of teams" to continually clarify key questions that communicate the heart and soul of an organization and its mission.

→ What is the state of the "container"—the holding environment of trusted relationships—for this change?

→ What is the charism we offer to the world as we change?

→ What is pain point calling for our charism in a world of change?

→ What is the transformation—*the deep change*—needed so we can offer our charism and fulfill our calling in the face of these problems in the world today?

Once again, leaders who have established their credibility through competence and have won the hard-earned trust of

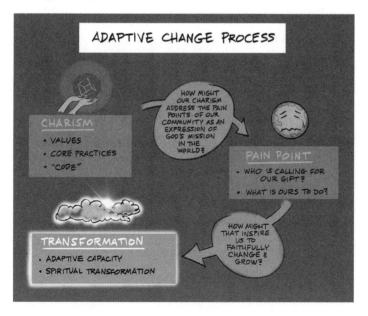

their people through their character and relational congruence do not rely on their trust and wisdom alone to navigate the change. They build in a team for the transformation. Adaptive leaders know that if "it takes a village to raise a child," then *"it takes a team to bring true transformation."*

> Adaptive change is deep change on the level of values, beliefs, and behavior.

One of my clients was thrust into a church leadership role when her senior pastor was abruptly asked to resign—right in the middle of a huge organizational transition process. Not only was the church in the midst of change but now they were without their leaders. My client, who had been one of the associate pastors, was being asked to shepherd the church through a very uncertain season. Frankly, most of the people in the pew assumed that she would just be a placeholder for a few days until a "real" interim pastor could be found. To her, it didn't matter if she was the associate pastor, the interim pastor, or the senior pastor. She just did the thing she does best: she gathered a team of colleagues together and they started collaborating—literally "co-laboring." Together they talked, prayed, planned, prayed some more, and talked even more. Soon a few days turned into a few weeks, a few weeks into a few months, and without fanfare, huge disruption, or significant financial cost, the church slowly moved into its future preparing for a new pastor. The anxious church calmed down and continued their organizational transition. What was this bold leadership move? *Convening a team.*[2]

She created an executive transformation team that could serve while the board functioned as a maintaining the mission group. Together this team of teams functioned as a holding environment of high trust to initiate and bring the transformation needed.

To invest trust in the deep change of transformation, a transformation team takes on the work of change with the authorized leader—including being a holding environment that contains the heat of change within the safety of strong relationships, protecting the organizational values, clarifying the organizational charism, and paying more attention to the actual pain points of the world that give the organization a true reason for being.

As the change process happens, the stakeholders who are most worried and most fearful are reassured that the changes are not the whims of one leader, but wise, thoughtful discernment by a diverse, representative, and trustworthy team of teams. They see that amid the necessary changes, what is most precious and important will be preserved. And they trust that if they are going to have to endure discomfort and disruption, the necessary changes are going to make a real difference in the world.

If change leaders are going to be able to simultaneously invest trust in transformation *and* learn to refill the trust accounts, at least three tasks need to be central to their leadership repertoire.

REGULATE THE HEAT

Perhaps the most important lesson for "disappointing people at a rate they can absorb" is to learn how to regulate the heat of transformation. Like a cook using a Dutch oven to make a hearty meal, for leadership expert John Kotter the pilot light for bringing transformational change is lit by "true urgency," that is, a "gut-level determination to move . . . now."[3] According to Kotter, 50 percent of organizational transformation endeavors that fail do so because the leaders did not create an appropriate sense of "true urgency." Without it there is no flame; no flame, no heat; no heat, nothing cooks—and no one is fed.

"True urgency" occurs when a group develops a clear conviction on the importance, opportunity, and necessity of the challenge in front of them. Kotter is careful to clarify that neither "complacency" nor "false urgency" is helpful here. Complacency— where everyone in the system believes that everything is "fine" and is resistant to change—is like a stove with no fire. Anxiety-ridden "false urgency"—where people are frantically working on issues that are not contributing to the real mission and needed transformation—is like having a sputtering pilot light that never really catches into a true, blue flame.

Because it is often difficult to distinguish between them, transformational leaders need to be careful not to confuse true urgency with their own or the system's anxiety, which will lead them to the quick fixes of false urgency instead of lasting change. The paradox is that it takes time and patience to create true urgency, which Heifetz and Linsky refer to as "letting an issue ripen":

> In your efforts to lead a community, you will often be thinking and acting ahead of them. But if you get too far ahead, raising issues before they are ready to be addressed, you create an opportunity for those you lead to sideline both you and the issue. You need to wait until the issue is ripe, or ripen it yourself. True, patience is not a virtue typically associated with people passionate about what they are doing. But holding off until the issue is ready may be critical in mobilizing people's energy and getting yourself heard. . . . *An issue becomes ripe when there is widespread urgency to deal with it*.[4]

Ask yourself, *Am I the only one who is losing sleep over the challenges that we face?* If so, then maybe you need to let this challenge ripen until there is true urgency, but if not—and if you have a motivated transformation team that is ready to move—then start turning up the heat by naming competing values.

> Transformational leaders need to be careful not to confuse true urgency with their own or the system's anxiety.

NAME AND NAVIGATE COMPETING VALUES

When my daughter was a little girl, she split her chin wide open jumping into a pool. She slipped on the slick deck, lost her footing, and hit the tile side. Within an hour we were in a doctor's office, and Ali was facing the painful necessity of stitches. Sure, the doctor was going to do his best to numb her chin and she didn't need many, but when she saw the needle coming toward her, she asked the doctor in a weepy voice, "Is this going to hurt?"

The doctor meant well. But he lied. "Oh no, this won't hurt at all."

And then it did. It didn't hurt as much at it could have without the anesthetic, but it certainly caused her pain. And she felt it. I saw her flinch and then saw her eyes fill with both tears and disappointment. I don't know what was worse, the needle or the betrayal.

It was a long time before my little girl stopped flinching in front of a doctor when she was hurt.

"If you can't name it, you can't navigate it," my colleague Michaela O'Donnell taught me when we were coteaching a doctoral cohort on leading change. At the heart of any painful transformational change are competing values. In adaptive change, leaders must very often go beyond finding "win-win solutions" to make necessary, hard decisions that will be required to move the mission forward.[5] Because the named values are genuinely *valuable*, the navigational pain of prioritizing one over another is inevitably experienced as deep loss, and often that loss feels to people like a "withdrawal" from the trust "account." Soon they are flinching whenever we come near them with a new idea.

> At the heart of any painful transformational change are competing values.

For leaders to ensure that the withdrawal becomes an investment in transformation rather than a squandering of a valuable resource, the competing values, the hard choices, and the missional necessity must be *honestly named*.

Let's be clear here also. If you make enough decisions that your people find painful, and you keep minimizing the pain, they'll stop trusting you. They'll flinch when you come near them like my daughter flinched with the doctor and the needle.

Giving in to the great temptation of trying to minimize the pain of decisions that feel like incisions, of "looking on the bright side" of something that requires a lament, or of minimizing the loss of having to let something valuable go, only leads to more mistrust. We have to learn to trust our people with the pain of change.

> **If you make enough decisions
> that your people find painful, and
> you keep minimizing the pain,
> they'll stop trusting you.**

The pain of choosing between good and valuable commitments; the sting of knowing that your particular preference isn't preferred at the moment; the discomfort of having a decision go against what you and your group think should be the priority—these experiences are always hard. They are always painful. There is no avoiding the pain. We can do everything possible to minimize it, but all change is experienced as loss, and loss is painful.

There is a paradox here. The more that leaders can name the pain of the hard decisions, the more trust they retain even when they are disappointing people. The more you name the competing values at stake and name them both as valuable, the more that others will be able to—eventually—trust you again. To invest trust in transformation requires trusting that you and your people can get through the pain of disappointment together.

> "If you can't name it, you can't navigate it."

TRUST AND THE TRANSFORMATION CYCLE

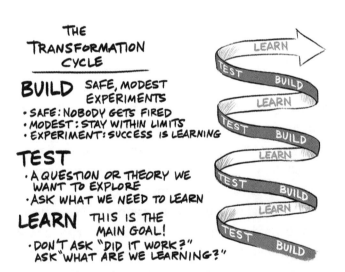

THE
TRANSFORMATION
CYCLE

BUILD SAFE, MODEST EXPERIMENTS
- SAFE: NOBODY GETS FIRED
- MODEST: STAY WITHIN LIMITS
- EXPERIMENT: SUCCESS IS LEARNING

TEST
- A QUESTION OR THEORY WE WANT TO EXPLORE
- ASK WHAT WE NEED TO LEARN

LEARN THIS IS THE MAIN GOAL!
- DON'T ASK "DID IT WORK?" ASK "WHAT ARE WE LEARNING?"

Since adaptive change is always about learning our way forward when there are no best practices from the past, adaptive leadership is fueled by experimentation. Good adaptive leaders learn how to keep the organization moving into uncharted territory by refueling trust *continually*; investing it wisely (and never squandering or hoarding it) with competence, congruence, and lots of communication; and continually conducting safe, modest experiments—what we call *prototypes*.[6]

When I was with the group of venture capitalists and entrepreneurs in Silicon Valley, they reminded me that experiments must be calibrated for the "minimum viable product." That is, when focusing on learning, make the experiments small, focused, simple, and easy to use so that you can maximize the amount of learning, discover a new question to explore, and repeat the cycle. Just as a smaller front chainring makes a bicycle easier to pedal (especially up a hill), completing a circle of learning as quickly as possible—and not at all worrying about the success—propels the learning process. "Fail fast, learn fast!" they exhorted me. To this, one venture capitalist blurted out, "And fail cheap! It's my money."

Everyone laughed and the point was made. Experimenting our way forward is an investment (of both money and trust!), but you shouldn't "spend down" either all at once. Safe, modest, simple, inexpensive experiments will help you focus on what you need to learn as quickly as possible, protect the investment of trust, and demonstrate to others that you are moving forward as wisely and prudently as possible.

THE ADAPTIVE RESET

The adaptive reset is to shift from relying on trust to learning to invest trust in transformation, reload the "trust account," and keep reinvesting the trust in transformation. This process of creating a holding environment of high trust relationships; clarifying and protecting the organizational charism; and paying attention to and focusing change work around a genuine pain point in the world enables the leadership team to invest trust in the deep change—the genuine transformation—that helps an organization to keep thriving in a changing world.

INVESTING TRUST IN TRANSFORMATION

1. CLARIFY YOUR CHARISM. HEALTH IS CLARITY.

2. PAY MORE ATTENTION TO COMMUNITY PAIN POINTS. WHAT PROBLEM IS CALLING TO US?

3. TALK TOGETHER OF THE TRANSFORMATION NEEDED. WHAT IS THE ADAPTIVE CHALLENGE FOR US IN THIS?

4. DON'T PREDICT. PROTOTYPE: WHAT QUESTIONS DO WE NEED TO EXPLORE ABOUT OUR OWN TRANSFORMATION?

5. REFUEL ON TRUST: KEEP GOING!

"Fail fast, learn fast!"

BALCONY
SESSION

① MAKE a LIST of the CHALLENGES that are KEEPING YOU UP at NIGHT. NEXT to THOSE CHALLENGES LIST the NAMES of ANYONE ELSE WHO FEELS the URGENCY of THOSE CHALLENGES as MUCH as YOU DO. IF YOU are the ONLY ONE FEELING the URGENCY of the PROBLEM, WHAT WOULD it MEAN to "LET it RIPEN"?

CHALLENGES

② WHAT are SOME WAYS that YOU CAN REGULATE the HEAT of a CHANGE PROCESS WHILE STILL NAMING the PAIN of NAVIGATING COMPETING VALUES?

③ WHAT ARE THREE THINGS YOU CAN DO — EVEN in the MIDST of a PAINFUL CHANGE PROCESS — THAT WOULD HELP REFUEL YOUR TRUST ACCOUNT?

TRUST

CHAPTER 7
THE STORY CONTINUES: BEYOND THE BOUQUETS & BALLOON SPRAYS

"Hi. I'm meeting Bob Phillips for lunch."

The manager of the Magnolia Country Club restaurant smiled warmly. "Of course, Dr. Grant. Nice to see you again. Mr. Phillips arrived a few minutes early and is at his usual table. Allow me to escort you."

As they walked through the casually elegant restaurant filled with seemingly important people either wearing suits or golf attire, Alison marveled at how she had become comfortable in navigating this world that was so foreign to her just a few years ago.

"There she is!" Bob rose from his chair to welcome her, both warmly familiar and somehow regal at the same time. "Our beloved leader!"

She hoped she hadn't blushed. "You make me sound like I'm the president of a country and not just the executive director of a nonprofit."

"*Just* an executive director! You're the leader of the organization that is responsible for more faith-based environmental science curriculum than anywhere in the South. When school boards and universities have backed away from teaching about climate change and the environment, you have made us relevant again. You did that. Your integrity and academic credibility won over so many donors, and your communication skills and ability to raise money have opened so many doors for our work. You are not just any executive director but the flesh-and-blood example of what Environmental Advocates is all about!"

Alison sat down at the table and put the cloth napkin in her lap. "Thank you, Bob. You're my best cheerleader. I really appreciate your support. Not every ED and chair have this kind of relationship, y' know?"

"It's because I trust you," he said as he took his seat again. "The board trusts you, and we're all committed to the same mission: 'Bringing science to the world to protect God's creation.' When a group of people can stack hands on the same mission, they can go far together."

"Yes. Exactly. That's why I wanted to have this lunch—and thank you for always hosting me here. It's such a beautiful setting and the food is so delicious. I'm really grateful."

Bob nodded. "Of course. The least I can do."

"It's also a good place, I think, for us to talk about the strategic planning process that I want to suggest to the board in two weeks. I'd really like us to see if we can 'stack

hands' on an adaptation that could only make our work more powerful."

He picked up his menu. "I know what you're going to say, Alison. I know you are going to suggest a change in our strategy, and I want you to know that I have begun to quietly talk to some board members. They are concerned that we are taking a turn from education to politics, and I think that if you even bring up the topic, those good feelings from the gala will disappear quickly."

Alison took a deep breath. "Bob, I really do appreciate the trust you all have in me. And that gala will be one of the lasting highlights of my career—of my life even—but good feelings are not what matters to me. You said it, our mission is 'Bringing science to the world to protect God's creation.' But what we actually do is bring *science to other science teachers who are already convinced*—I know! I was one of them. We have created a well-endowed echo chamber that creates lots of good feelings among a few Christian teachers and donors who want to support science, but it isn't moving the needle. I just want us to have a candid conversation about what we mean when we say 'the world.'"

She might not get another moment like this with him. This was her chance to make her case. "We are Environmental Advocates, Bob. We advocate. For the past generation that has meant funding research and curriculum for those who want to advocate for protecting the environment as an expression of their Christian faith, but I just want to ask whether we should be supporting and training these advocates in every sector. I want us to begin a thoughtful process of examining what it would mean for us to fund research *and* support those who will also take that research into places where it could make a difference. I want to change the model from the teacher in the classroom to teams of smart and capable people who are engaging the environmental challenges in every sector of society. I want us to fund and support and recruit—"

Bob cut her off mid-sermon. "Oh, I agree with you. I do. If it were up to me, we would do like you say. But to many of our donors, it feels like we're crossing into politics. It's so controversial. I can't even imagine the press we'll receive. It may turn off the very donors we need to keep us afloat. Your plan is a huge gamble. The very people who trust you now and give to us could turn against us. The very research we fund could be at risk!"

She knew he was trying to protect her. She could also hear the fear in his voice. Bob had given a lot to this work. He was a researcher himself who had gone on to make a small fortune on a technology that he had sold to an automobile manufacturer. His faith was in the power of research to change minds.

"Bob, what I am suggesting is nothing more than what you did. You are my model here. You took your research into the marketplace, and it changed a lot of minds in the automotive industry. But don't you think we could be making it easier for other researchers who didn't have your family connections?"

Bob winced. She had cut a little too close to home. She rushed to reassure him. "I'm not saying that your research wouldn't have been accepted on its merits alone. I'm just saying that every good idea needs a *team* of advocates—just like you had. And especially in spaces that have become more resistant to our environmental commitments, we need to re-cruit, resource, and support advocates who can work with researchers to make a real difference everywhere.

"Just like you and I are a good team with donors and community leaders, researchers like us need teammates. Can you think of how we could get our donors and board members to shift from seeing themselves as patrons to seeing themselves as partners? *Real* partners . . . with researchers . . . and teachers . . . and lawyers . . . and journalists . . . and writers . . . and artists . . . and pastors . . . and politicians?"

Bob chuckled. "I guess if it takes a village to raise a child, it might take a team to save the earth!"

She smiled at her mentor. "I can lead this change, Bob. I believe in it, and I believe I have earned the right to try. You've seen what I can do to get our organization back on its feet. And we can go on raising money, giving out scholarships, and funding papers to be read at conferences, where—let's face it—nobody is really paying attention.

"But if we are going to figure out how to truly educate both the church and the world, I will need your help. I will need you to talk to the board members and donors when they get nervous. I will need someone who can hear the pushback and keep the relationships strong until we get buy-in. I will need you to help me recruit others to join our little band of change agents. To truly transform this organization into a 'team of teams' that makes a difference in the world, it'll have to start with you and me being partners leading our team."

She looked him in the eye. "Will you join me? Can we stack hands on trying this together?"

Bob held her gaze a moment, then looked away to signal a nearby server. "Excuse me," he said. "Could we get a small split of champagne for lunch? We're celebrating a new partnership."

BALCONY SESSION

1. FOR THIS FINAL BALCONY SESSION, CONSIDER ALISON GRANT WALKING INTO that MEETING WITH HER BOARD CHAIRPERSON — WHAT do YOU IMAGINE SHE was FEELING? WHAT do YOU IMAGINE was HER INNER DIALOGUE WHEN SHE was PREPARING for the MEETING?

2. WHICH PEOPLE in YOUR ORGANIZATION do YOU NEED to ENGAGE as PART of a TRUSTED TRANSFORMATION TEAM? WHAT do YOU NEED to DO to STRENGTHEN the RELATIONSHIPS on that TEAM so it COULD be a GOOD HOLDING ENVIRONMENT?

3. WHAT DO YOU ANTICIPATE WILL be the FIRST CHALLENGE for YOUR TRANSFORMATION TEAM to INVEST TRUST in TRANSFORMATION?

4. WHICH of the SKILLSETS are MOST IMPORTANT for YOU to DEVELOP so YOU CAN BOTH BRING TRANSFORMATION & REFILL on TRUST?

ACKNOWLEDGMENTS

This series of small books is the result of countless conversations and consultations over the last fifteen years with dedicated leaders who cared so much about their organizations that they invested deeply in their own transformation. Thank you all for trusting me and letting me walk alongside you.

These also are the first books I have written since I started AE Sloan Leadership in 2021 with my wife, Beth, and Angela Bae Williams. I want to acknowledge them as my partners and teammates, as well as Ali Gradert and Erin Zillner, who make doing this work so meaningful and so incredibly fun. They, along with our first senior coaches, Linda Roberts and Daniel White, were the wise, caring voices represented in the learnings presented here.

In addition, several experienced leaders allowed me to interview them to more deeply understand the nuances of everything from running a small business and leading in a prison to running a nonprofit and mastering jujitsu. To Mike Bollenbacher, Chris Dolkas, Mark Gradert, Michaela O'Donnell, Nicholas Firkin, David Hallgren, Matt Miller, Robert Perales, Kelly Padgett, and Joshua Serrano, thank you for your generosity and insight.

These books were also one of the most satisfying experiences of collaboration and creativity that I have ever experienced. I am deeply indebted to my editor, Cindy Bunch, and her outstanding team at InterVarsity Press. Thank you, Cindy, Ted Olsen, Lisa Renninger, and Sharon Brown, my fiction coach. You all went the extra mile for an author who had a wild idea about a little series of books that he had never seen anywhere else.

To my agent, Kathy Helmers, for being a champion, cheerleader, and coach—I can truly say that these books would not have been possible without you.

To Mark Demel, my incredible illustrator: your capacity to capture my words into what I can't even see and make it clearer and cleverer than I could ever imagine seems like magic. It is certainly a gift—as was working with you.

To Marty Linsky: your leadership work has been the foundation for all of mine. Meeting you was a professional and personal highlight, and the meals and conversations were such a gift that I practically levitate telling people about it. Your willingness to write the foreword for these books is an honor. I am humbled and grateful.

Lastly, these books of lessons that I have learned in coaching others all began with my own coaches and mentors teaching me. To Jim Osterhaus, Steve Yamaguchi, and Terry Looper, this dedication is way too small of a way of expressing the enormity of my thanks.

DISCUSSION GUIDE
TAKE YOUR TEAM TO THE BALCONY

Now that you have worked your way through this book and engaged in your own "balcony work," it's time to take your team to the balcony and practice together in real time on one of the challenges that you are facing right now.

We suggest that you set aside two to three hours (or even a half-day retreat) to take up this exercise together. Everyone who is participating should have read this book ahead of time.

As we have already learned, change leaders need a process that will enable them to engage people in their own transformation at the right pace and without wasting the time or opportunity necessary for the transformation to occur. *The old mindset of storing up trust must give way to a new adaptive reset of investing trust in transformation.*

This process starts with a team of teams functioning as a holding environment that is strong and safe because of the good, trusting relationships experienced within the group. When leaders create a holding environment for making the important decisions, the other stakeholders in the organization can trust that the transformation needed is being shaped by the genuine work of discernment held by a trustworthy team.

This group balcony session focuses on strengthening the team into a holding environment. Please ask each person who is coming to the gathering to be prepared with their answers to these questions:

1. Review the Margaret Wheatley quote that started this book: "It is possible to prepare for the future without knowing what it will be. The primary way to prepare for the unknown is to attend to the quality of our relationships, to how well we know and trust one another."[1]

2. How would you describe the quality of our relationships and "how well we know and trust each other" on this team?

3. On a scale of one to five (one meaning "it is very hard to trust each other" and five meaning "I have complete trust in this team"), where would you say your trust level is right now?

4. How hard is it to name your level of trust out loud in front of the team?

5. What are the dynamics or agreements that we could work on that would strengthen our trust in each other? What do you personally need to be able to better know and trust the others on this team?

When the group comes together, review the quote from Margaret Wheatley and then ask each person to personally check in on each of the four questions (one at a time) that we asked them to prepare ahead of time.

Then discuss this additional line and the following questions:

1. In the same interview about trust and relationships, Margaret Wheatley added, "There is one core principle for developing these relationships. People must be engaged in meaningful work together if they are to transcend individual concerns and develop new capacities."[2]

2. What is one way that you have experienced our relational trust and capacity for working together growing through "meaningful work together"?

3. If "our meaningful work together" is to lead this organization through change together, what agreements and practices do we need to strengthen our trust as a holding environment?

4. What else do you think we need to grow in our trust and the quality of our relationships together?

NOTES

ABOUT THE PRACTICING CHANGE SERIES

[1] I have written extensively about adaptive leadership in *Canoeing the Mountains: Leading in Uncharted Territory* (Downers Grove, IL: InterVarsity Press, 2015). See this definition on page 19:

> Adaptive challenges are the true tests of leadership. They are challenges that go beyond the technical solutions of resident experts or best practices, or even the organization's current knowledge. They arise when the world around us has changed but we continue to live on the successes of the past. They are challenges that cannot be solved through compromise or win-win scenarios, or by adding another ministry or staff person to the team. They demand that leaders make hard choices about what to preserve and to let go. They are challenges that require people to learn and to change, that require leaders to experience and navigate profound loss.

See also Ronald A. Heifetz and Marty Linsky, *Leadership on the Line: Staying Alive Through the Dangers of Leading* (Boston, MA: Harvard Business, 2002), 13.

[2] See also Ronald Heifetz, Marty Linsky, and Alexander Grashow, *The Practice of Adaptive Leadership: Tools and Tactics for Changing Your Organization and the World* (Boston, MA: Harvard Business, 2009), loc. 340, Kindle.

[3] As Richard Rohr has famously written, "We do not think ourselves into new ways of living, we live ourselves into new ways of thinking." Richard Rohr, *Everything Belongs: The Gift of Contemplative Prayer*, rev. and updated ed. (1999; repr. New York: Crossroad, 2003), loc. 129, Kindle.

[4] These case studies are all fictionalized versions of actual problems that either I or my clients faced. I have changed all identifying features and conflated a few similar stories into a single narrative, but these case studies represent real-life challenges.

[5]To be sure, I am following the pattern that was introduced by Heifetz, Linsky, and Grashow, *Practice of Adaptive Leadership*. I am indebted to these authors for their fine work and am adapting it for a different context that works primarily with faith-based, nonprofit, and mission agency leadership.

[6]"Achieving a balcony perspective means taking yourself out of the dance, in your mind, even if only for a moment." Heifetz and Linsky, *Leadership on the Line*, loc. 760, Kindle. See also Heifetz, Linsky, and Grashow, *Practice of Adaptive Leadership*, loc. 282, Kindle.

INTRODUCTION

[1]Tod Bolsinger, *Canoeing the Mountains: Leading in Uncharted Territory* (Downers Grove, IL: InterVarsity Press, 2015), 35.

[2]Ronald Heifetz, Marty Linsky, and Alexander Grashow, *The Practice of Adaptive Leadership: Tools and Tactics for Changing Your Organization and the World* (Boston, MA: Harvard Business, 2009), loc. 2177, Kindle.

[3]See Marty Linsky, "Leadership on the Line: Staying Alive Through the Dangers of Leading," interview with Martha Lagace, Working Knowledge, May 28, 2002, https://hbswk.hbs.edu/archive/leadership-on-the-line -staying-alive-through-the-dangers-of-leading.

[4]Ronanld A. Heifetz and Marty Linsky, *Leadership on the Line: Staying Alive Through the Dangers of Leading* (Boston, MA: Harvard Business, 2002), 11-12.

2. OLD MINDSET

[1]Margaret Wheatley, "When Change Is Out of Our Control," published in *Human Resources in the 21st Century* (Hoboken, NJ: Wiley, 2003), accessed July 31, 2023, www.margaretwheatley.com/articles/whenchangeisout ofcontrol.html.

[2]See David Brooks, "America is Having a Moral Convulsion," *Atlantic*, October 5, 2020, www.theatlantic.com/ideas/archive/2020/10/collapsing -levels-trust-are-devastating-america/616581/. Compare to Lee Rainie, Scott Keeter, and Andrew Perrin, "Trust and Distrust in America," *Pew Research Center*, July 22, 2019, www.pewresearch.org/politics/2019/07/22 /trust-and-distrust-in-america/.

[3]J. R. Woodward, *The Scandal of Leadership: Unmasking the Powers of Domination in the Church* (Cody, WY: 100 Movements Publishing, 2023).

[4]From a phone interview conducted by the author with Jim Osterhaus in June 2011. Originally printed in Tod Bolsinger, *Canoeing the Mountains: Leading in Uncharted Territory* (Downers Grove, IL: InterVarsity Press, 2015), 69.

[5]Bolsinger, *Canoeing the Mountains*, 42-44.

[6]With thanks to my colleague Scott Cormode for this memorable and inspiring reframe of the people who have often just been called "followers." Scott Cormode, "A People Entrusted to Your Care," *Fuller Magazine* 10, n.d., accessed September 1, 2023, https://fullerstudio.fuller.edu /a-people-entrusted-to-your-care/.

[7]I first wrote about this in some depth in Bolsinger, *Canoeing the Mountains*, chapters 3–5.

[8]Stephen M. R. Covey with Rebecca Merrill, *The Speed of Trust: The One Thing That Changes Everything* (New York: Free Press, 2006), loc. 527-28, Kindle.

[9]See John Kotter, "What Leaders Really Do," *Harvard Business Review*, December 2001, https://hbr.org/2001/12/what-leaders-really-do. "Leadership and management are two distinctive and complementary systems of action. Each has its own function and characteristic activities. Both are necessary for success in an increasingly complex and volatile business environment."

[10]Kotter, "What Leaders Really Do."

[11]See Bolsinger, *Canoeing the Mountains*, 43-44.

[12]Ronald Heifetz, Marty Linsky, and Alexander Grashow, *The Practice of Adaptive Leadership: Tools and Tactics for Changing Your Organization and the World* (Boston, MA: Harvard Business, 2009), loc. 340, Kindle.

3. NEW SKILLSET PART 1

[1]Adapted from Tod Bolsinger, *Canoeing the Mountains: Leading in Uncharted Territory* (Downers Grove, IL: InterVarsity Press, 2015), 161.

[2]Ronald A. Heifetz and Marty Linsky, *Leadership on the Line: Staying Alive Through the Dangers of Leading* (Boston, MA: Harvard Business, 2002), 13.

[3]Ronald Heifetz, "Leadership, Adaptability, and Thriving," Convocation & Pastors School at Duke Divinity School, October 14, 2008, posted by Faith & Leadership, www.youtube.com/watch?v=CSZld1VlYxc (emphasis mine).

[4]A "holding environment" is defined as

> the cohesive properties of a relationship or social system that serve to keep people engaged with one another in spite of the divisive forces generated by adaptive work. May include, for example, bonds of affiliation and love; agreed-on rules, procedures, and norms; shared purposes and common values; traditions, language, and rituals; familiarity with adaptive work; and trust in authority. Holding environments give a group identity and contain the conflict, chaos, and confusion often produced when struggling with complex problematic realities.

Ronald Heifetz, Marty Linsky, and Alexander Grashow, *The Practice of Adaptive Leadership: Tools and Tactics for Changing Your Organization and the World* (Boston, MA: Harvard Business, 2009), loc. 4936-41, Kindle.

[5]Heifetz, Linsky, and Grashow, *Practice of Adaptive Leadership*, loc. 2567-70, Kindle.

[6]In *Canoeing the Mountains*, I referred to this as crock-pot leadership, but in talking to leaders they challenged the idea that real change could come over a period of time in a perfectly safe environment that you could practically ignore. I started talking about using a big Dutch oven with its need for attention, observation, stirring, and regulating the heat. In addition, a Dutch oven—if you are not careful—can certainly burn you too!

[7]General Stanley McChrystal, with Tantum Collins, David Silverman, and Chris Fussell, *Team of Teams: New Rules of Engagement for a Complex World* (New York, NY: Penguin, 2015), 2.

[8]McChrystal et al., *Team of Teams*, 20.

[9]This section is adapted from Bolsinger, *Canoeing the Mountains*, 165.

[10]This section is adapted from Bolsinger, *Canoeing the Mountains*, 167-68.

[11]Heifetz, Linsky, and Grashow, *Practice of Adaptive Leadership*, loc. 383, Kindle.

[12]Michaela O'Donnell, interview with the author, August 8, 2023.

[13]Dave Gibbons, cited in Bolsinger, *Canoeing the Mountains*, 199.

4. NEW SKILLSET PART 2

[1]Wendell Berry, "Some Further Words," *New Collected Poems* (Berkeley, CA: Counterpoint, 2012), 362.

[2]For more on this, see Tod Bolsinger, *Leading Through Resistance: Quit Pushing Back*, Practicing Change Series (Downers Grove, IL: InterVarsity Press, 2024).

[3]For more on the dual convictions needed to bring healthy adaptive change, see Tod Bolsinger, *The Mission Always Wins: Quit Appeasing Stakeholders*, Practicing Change Series (Downers Grove, IL: InterVarsity Press, 2024).

[4]"Contrary to popular wisdom, the proper first response to a changing world is not to ask, 'How should we change?' but rather to ask, 'What do we stand for and why do we exist?' This should never change. And *then* feel free to change everything else." Jim Collins and Jerry I. Porras, *Built to Last*, 3rd ed., Good to Great book 2 (New York: HarperBusiness, 2011), loc. 79, Kindle.

[5]For more on why this popular advice often creates more problems than it solves, see Tod Bolsinger, "What to Do When We Don't Know Where We Are Going," *Fuller Magazine* 24, January 2023, https://fuller studio.fuller.edu/theology/what-to-do-when-we-dont-know-where -we-are-going/.

[6]See Ori Brafman and Rod A. Beckstrom, "In Search of the Sweet Spot," chapter 8 of *The Starfish and the Spider: The Unstoppable Power of Leaderless Organizations* (New York: Penguin, 2006; emphasis mine). For more insight in how this applies in faith-based organizations, see Tod Bolsinger, *Canoeing the Mountains: Leading in Uncharted Territory* (Downers Grove, IL: InterVarsity Press, 2015), loc. 790, Kindle.

[7]"DNA," Wikipedia, http://en.wikipedia.org/wiki/DNA.

[8]Kevin G. Ford, *Transforming Church: Bringing Out the Good to Get to Great* (Colorado Springs: David C. Cook, 2008), loc. 915-16, Kindle.

[9]Ronald Heifetz, "Leadership, Adaptability, and Thriving," Convocation & Pastors School at Duke Divinity School, October 14, 2008, posted by Faith & Leadership, www.youtube.com/watch?v=CSZId1VlYxc (emphasis mine).

[10]Bolsinger, *Canoeing the Mountains*, loc. 790, Kindle.

[11]Brené Brown, "Research," brenebrown.com, n.d., https://brenebrown .com/the-research/, accessed November 13, 2023.

[12]With gratitude to Father Daniel Dorsey, the president of the Glenmary Home Missioners, an order of the Catholic Church, for sharing his unpublished paper on monastic orders and charism with me. The paper has been reproduced on the Glenmary Home Missioners website as an article, "The Theological Concept of the Charism of a Founder," https:// glenmary.org/our-story/our-founders-vision-mission/father-bishops -charism/the-theological-concept-of-the-charism-of-a-founder/, accessed November 19, 2023.

[13]See the description of Benedictine spirituality of Holy Wisdom Monastery in Madison, WI, "Benedictine Spirituality in the 21st Century," Holy Wisdom Monastery, May 5, 2011, https://holywisdommonastery.org /benedictine-spirituality-in-the-21-century/.

[14]"Loyola described the ideal Jesuit as 'living with one foot raised'— always ready to respond to emerging opportunities." Chris Lowney, *Heroic Leadership: Best Practices from a 450-Year-Old Company That Changed the World* (Chicago: Loyola Press, 2009), 29. For a brief description of Jesuit leadership see Chris Lowney, "Who Are Our Leaders?," jesuitresource.org, February 16, 2005, www.xavier.edu/jesuitresource /jesuit-a-z/documents/who-are-our-leaders.

[15]Tod Bolsinger, "The Deep Satisfaction of Accomplishing Something Together," an interview of Gordon T. Smith, *Christianity Today*, February 8, 2018, www.christianitytoday.com/ct/2018/february-web-only/deep -satisfaction-of-accomplishing-something-together.html.

5. NEW SKILLSET PART 3

[1]Tod E. Bolsinger, *Tempered Resilience*, Tempered Resilience Set (Downers Grove, IL: InterVarsity Press, 2020), 18-19.

[2]I originally discussed this in Bolsinger, *Tempered Resilience*, 155.

[3]I originally shared this story in Bolsinger, *Tempered Resilience*, 14-17.

[4]Mark Wingfield, "Baylor Joins the Nation's Academic Elite as a Research 1 University," Baptist News Global, December 16, 2021, https://baptistnews .com/article/baylor-joins-the-nations-academic-elite-as-a-research -1-university/.

[5]Todd Copeland, "A World of Good," *Baylor Magazine*, Summer 2022, www .baylor.edu/alumni/magazine/2004/index.php?id=985232.

6. ADAPTIVE RESET

[1]James P. Osterhaus, Joseph M. Jurkowski, and Todd A. Hahn, *Thriving Through Ministry Conflict* (Grand Rapids, MI: Zondervan, 2009), 84.

[2]"In communal transformation, leadership is about intention, convening, valuing relatedness, and presenting choices." Peter Block, *Community: The Structure of Belonging* (Oakland, CA: Berrett-Koehler, 2018), loc. 977-78, Kindle. I shared this story originally in Tod E. Bolsinger, *Canoeing the Mountains* (Downers Grove, IL: InterVarsity Press, 2015), 67-68.

[3]"Our Foundation: The 8 Steps for Leading Change," Kotter International, n.d., accessed November 13, 2023, www.kotterinternational .com/our-principles/changesteps/step-1.

[4]Ronald A. Heifetz and Marty Linsky, *Leadership on the Line: Staying Alive Through the Dangers of Leading* (Boston, MA: Harvard Business, 2002), 146 (emphasis mine).

[5]For a deeper dive on the limits of a win-win perspective see Tod Bolsinger, *The Mission Always Wins: Quit Appeasing Stakeholders*, Practicing Change Series (Downers Grove, IL: InterVarsity Press, 2024).

[6]This process of learning through creating prototypes is described in detail in Tod Bolsinger, *How Not to Waste a Crisis: Quit Trying Harder*, Practicing Change Series (Downers Grove, IL: InterVarsity Press, 2024).

DISCUSSION GUIDE

[1]Margaret Wheatley, "When Change Is Out of Our Control," published in *Human Resources in the 21st Century* (Hoboken, NJ: Wiley, 2003), accessed July 31, 2023, www.margaretwheatley.com/articles/whenchangeisoutof control.html.

[2]Wheatley, "When Change Is Out of Our Control."

The Practicing Change Series

How Not to Waste a Crisis
978-1-5140-0866-9

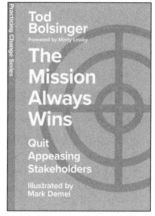

The Mission Always Wins
978-1-5140-0868-3

Leading Through Resistance
978-1-5140-0870-6

Invest in Transformation
978-1-5140-0872-0

Also Available

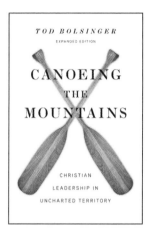

Canoeing the Mountains, Expanded Edition
978-0-8308-4147-9

Tempered Resilience
978-0-8308-4164-6